FIRSTBORN

FIRSTBORN

a memoir

lauren christensen

PENGUIN PRESS

NEW YORK

2025

PENGUIN PRESS
An imprint of Penguin Random House LLC
1745 Broadway, New York, NY 10019
penguinrandomhouse.com

Designed by Christina Nguyen

LIBRARY OF CONGRESS CATALOGING-IN-PUBLICATION DATA
Names: Christensen, Lauren, 1967– author.
Title: Firstborn / Lauren Christensen.
Description: New York : Penguin Press, 2025. | Summary: "A memoir of love,
familial bonds, and grief that defies consolation, which the author began
writing the day she lost her daughter in utero" —Provided by publisher.
Identifiers: LCCN 2024013329 (print) | LCCN 2024013330 (ebook) |
ISBN 9780593831816 (hardcover) | ISBN 9780593831823 (ebook)
Subjects: LCSH: Stillbirth—Psychological aspects. | Christensen, Lauren, 1967– |
Fetal death—New York (State)—New York. | Mothers—North Carolina—
Chapel Hill—Biography. | Pregnant women—North Carolina—
Chapel Hill—Biography. | Loss (Psychology) | Motherhood. |
Christensen, Lauren, 1967– —Family.
Classification: LCC RG635.U62 N73 2025 (print) | LCC RG635.U62 (ebook) |
DDC 155.937085—dc23/eng/20241024
LC record available at https://lccn.loc.gov/2024013329
LC ebook record available at https://lccn.loc.gov/2024013330

Printed in the United States of America
1st Printing

The authorized representative in the EU for product safety and compliance
is Penguin Random House Ireland, Morrison Chambers, 32 Nassau Street,
Dublin D02 YH68, Ireland, https://eu-contact.penguin.ie.

For Simone

Hear me out: that which you call death
I remember.

—Louise Glück, *The Wild Iris*

The fear is for what is still to be lost.
You may see nothing still to be lost.
Yet there is no day in her life on which
I do not see her.

—Joan Didion, *Blue Nights*

FIRSTBORN

Some days I still think this is all just a sad story I'll tell Simone one day.

That when the crying nurse brought her to me, brought her body to me, still in the hospital bed, an epidural and an IV and a catheter still inside me and a blood pressure monitor still Velcroed around my right bicep, I'd just taken a bite of a banana.

That it was the first solid food I'd eaten in twenty hours, the obstetrician having been uncertain whether I'd need an emergency cesarean section, in which case I couldn't have anything in my stomach. I hadn't needed a cesarean, and now everything was over, and I was hungry.

That when I saw the bundle of white cloth in the nurse's arms, I instinctively handed the half-eaten banana to my husband, so I could reach out my arms for her. She was even more heavily swaddled than most newborns because the doctors and nurses hadn't wanted me to see the swelling that had accumulated around her head and back, inside her abdomen, underneath her skin. "Are you sure you want to see her?" the obstetrician, Doctor R, had asked after pulling Simone from my body, stillborn and breech, at twenty-two weeks' gestation. Her voice was gentle and deep, and she held both of my hands in hers. "There is a lot of swelling."

I understood she was only trying to prepare me, this mother of daughters—"I have a Lauren at home too," she'd told my mother the previous morning, when we'd met for the first time in her creaky Upper East Side office. I understood that she only needed to hear me say it: There was nothing in the world that could keep me from her. I was not afraid to see my child.

It was just like everyone had said it would be, and it was nothing like that. Seeing her face—the only part of her I could see, underneath a white cotton hat with a little pom-pom on it, an impossibly small hat that was so big on her it threatened to swallow her whole head—felt like coming home to a loved one after a long trip, lonely and exhausting, somewhere far away. Oh, it's you.

Of course, her face was familiar in a more literal sense too. The wide, high brow bones, the soft lips upturned slightly at the edges, the angular little nose: She looked, entirely and miraculously, like her dad.

I kissed her forehead and cheek, put my nose to her skin and breathed her in. She smelled, perhaps unsurprisingly, like me. She felt weightless in my arms—her little hospital bracelet read one pound, two ounces, thirty centimeters—and I imagined continuing to carry her around with me, physically I mean, for the rest of my life: to work, to dinner with my friends, to weddings and vacations and funerals and the grocery store and my deathbed. I could do it, I thought. It would take no effort at all.

I passed her to Gabe, and he walked around the room staring at her, bouncing her a little as if she needed soothing, as if she needed anything at all from us now. She looked even smaller against his chest, a tiny, endangered bird he'd found and rescued, cradling her until he returned her safely to the nest.

You were still warm, I'll tell her one day. Your eyes were closed; you did not cry. You were peaceful. You were the only perfect thing I have ever done.

Later, I would try to imagine how Simone would have looked in a year, in five, in forty; what her voice would have sounded like, her laugh, her cry. But in those few minutes I had with her, I took her in just as she was. Her father and I passed her gently between us, again and again, not just smiling but beaming. "One more time, I just want to hold her one more time," we said, until the nurse took her away, and our arms were empty.

Somehow, this memory is still the happiest of my life.

I will never get to tell Simone this story; the person I most need to hear it never will. It is an intolerable reality that I have outlived my only child, that what cells remain of her are collected in an oppressively small porcelain urn on the dresser beside our bed, a frail vessel painted white with a bird and branches on it, the lid sealed only with Scotch tape because the funeral home wasn't sure, we weren't sure, whether we'd planned to scatter her ashes or preserve them. That no matter what we do with them, those cells will never develop or multiply enough to comprehend such things as fear or urns or sadness or stories. Stories like this one are for the rest of us, the ones left behind.

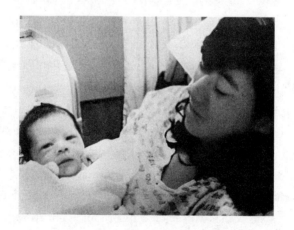

Simone was the fourth generation of women in my family. I have no photo of her, because I didn't want to take one, but these are the photos I do have. In the earlier image, the grandmother is not yet a grandmother; she has only just become a mother. It is September 1958, and her first child, a girl, is three days old. They are together in a bed and in black-and-white, at their small apartment in Toronto, the infant's head making the wrinkled pillow behind it look comically, almost menacingly large, a parody of a pillow, how could a head ever need so much pillow?

This head, the center of the frame, turns toward her mother's smiling face gazing down at her from the top-left corner, looking for her milk, maybe, a flower turning toward the sun.

Thirty-one years later, there is a new photo. The original is in color, it is late August 1989, and the baby girl from before now has her own. This new baby is jaundiced but healthy, seven pounds and seven ounces, round-faced and hairy. The mother is wearing a hospital-issued gown with a bunch of Ns on it for some reason (the hospital is called Pacific Presbyterian), and her shoulder-length black hair is swept across her forehead. In this photo, a rare one taken of the mother without makeup, she is peaceful, enamored, exhausted, and so, so tan. Her beauty is undeniable, particularly in this moment. She too stares straight down at her daughter.

This baby's hands are in small fists held right up at her chin, and her dark, wrinkled eyes are not looking toward her mother. They stare straight at the camera, maybe at whoever is behind it—the father? The grandmother?

There is no photo after this one. Where is this daughter's daughter? Whom does she have to look at?

This baby is the mother's second. The first time around, she marveled at how much easier pregnancy had turned out to be than she'd been led to expect. At how fortunate she was to feel so well all the time, so exempt from the bone-deep exhaustion and roiling nausea all her less fortunate friends complained about while carrying. It eventually became clear that she, this mother, was the unlucky one. That baby, a boy, died inside of her at nearly six months' gestation. When she found out his heart had stopped, the mother felt like hers did too.

A little over a year later, they bring the girl home to a town house in the Pacific Heights neighborhood of San Francisco, a block away from a playground at the top of a steep hill, which the girl will eventually love so much she refuses to leave, where she will wail when her nanny, a short-haired woman who speaks to her only in Mandarin, tries in vain to get her to leave.

The house has a little balcony in the back where the mother makes the father, a lapsed Mormon, go to smoke. He wears big, square, wire-framed glasses, and a well-worn short-sleeved button-down in a kind of geometric vomit of bright turquoises and blues. Still, he is handsome; people say he looks like Christopher Reeve. He is tall and charismatic and speaks with the earnestness of good intention, and the mother fell in love with him after meeting him one time in a stairwell, in 1984. They wrote love letters back and forth across the country for months. He has family money and an MBA; she has neither of these things but a decently paying merchandising job and a mind like a lit match. They were married within a year.

On a windy day in February when the daughter is twenty-eight, the mother will take her back to that house, will ignore the daughter's mortification and knock on the door, ask the new owner if she can come in, she's come from all the way across the country, from New York, to show her daughter her first home. The woman who answers the door will be significantly older than the mother; her husband is the city's former mayor. An American flag will flap out front. She'll look at the mother and daughter, their shin-length felt coats, one black and one pale pink, their sunglasses and large shopping bags. She'll welcome them inside.

Standing uneasily in the long, narrow, mahogany-paneled sitting room on the ground floor, the mother will say to the woman, "Those tiles in the bathroom upstairs toward the back of the house, the ones with the blue trim? Are they still there?"

When she was pregnant the second time, you see, emotional and impulsive and two weeks overdue in the dead of August, the thing she felt she needed to do most urgently was to retile the bathroom that accompanied her unborn child's bedroom. "My baby can't have plain tiles," she'd said to the father. They bought the tiles.

"Those? We haven't changed them," the woman will tell the mother, nearly three decades later. They can't go upstairs, the cleaning ladies are there, the woman apologizes, hopes they don't mind. The daughter will never get to see the tiles, but it won't really matter. Knowing they ever existed, and still exist, despite everything, will be enough. In some ways, the image she will always carry in her mind, of this bathroom, this life, will be truer than the reality anyway.

By then the father will also live far away from that house, in a seaside apartment right off the 5, halfway between Los Angeles and San Diego. All three will live in their separate apartments, a molecule atomized, each forming new bonds with new loved ones. As the years pass the mother will think about the father less and less; the daughter will think of him more and more.

Whenever she is sad, for example, or sick, or hurt, she will wonder how he'd react if he knew. As she grows older, that curiosity and longing will calcify into resentment. She will try to imagine one day having a child of her own, and then not even knowing or asking how or where that child is for months, even years at a time. She will wonder if it matters to him that she's safe—in her most ungenerous moments, that she's alive. How long it would take him to find out if she weren't.

It will never be entirely clear to the daughter what happened after the time of the blue-trimmed tiles. Something about the father—who, unlike the mother, grew up with a silver spoon, the mother's mother always said—quitting his consulting job to go on a motorcycle trip around the country, leaving his wife at home to take care of their infant child.

When the mother and daughter are living in Dallas a few years later—these will be some of the daughter's first memories—the mother will meet an older man, a retail CEO who lives in New York City and is everything the father is not: cautious, reliable, present to a fault. The man will visit them and take the three-year-old daughter swimming in the pool at his hotel. Afterward, the girl's arms rubbed raw from her water wings, they'll sit on lounge chairs and order French fries, which the man will call "feijis," an approximation of the Mandarin word for airplane, and when a plane passes overhead he'll point to the sky and say, "Look, a French fry!" The daughter will laugh and laugh and the mother will think, This is what the two of them need: someone to count on.

She'll move to the Upper East Side and marry him; the daughter, makeup covering her chickenpox, will be the flower girl. First there will be the hotel on Sixty-First Street, where the daughter will have two goldfish that will die when the family goes to Florida for a week in March. Then the apartment four blocks north, where the girl will wet her bed and put on a plaid school jumper and sing "Dreamlover" into the mirror and have her first panic attack at six.

Around that time, the father will visit New York for work, and he will take his daughter out to dinner at an expensive Chinese restaurant near her home. They won't have much time together; he'll have to bring the girl back to the only family she knows in just a few hours. When they walk in, the maître d' will recognize the girl, and call her by the stepfather's last name. It will bother the daughter more than it bothers the father. He's not possessive like that, he understands. He'll already know she does not belong to him; what she knows is that she does not belong to the stepfather either. She is her mother's alone, always.

Soon the mother, the daughter, and the stepfather will fly from New York to Baton Rouge to meet the son, a pale and hairless string bean of a baby, just two weeks old, in a foster home in Mamou, Louisiana, where he's lived his two weeks on earth since the fifteen-year-old girl felt she had no choice but to let him go. The daughter, now eight, will be the first to hold her new brother, sitting on that kind foster family's brown couch in her purple chenille sweater over a white cotton turtleneck. She'll continue to hold him in her arms as they both fall asleep on the flight back up to their new life.

Soon that marriage will end too. Lying on her stomach on top of the mother's white embroidered bedspread, the ten-year-old daughter will listen to the mother tell her they'll be leaving this home, this man too. This time, she'll be old enough to remember, to betray her mother by running into the den late at night, where the stepfather is watching television on a black leather armchair, climbing into his lap, and telling him she's sorry for everything the mother has ever done.

During all this time the girl will see her father once every couple of years, will seldom hear from him in between. When she is very young, she will regard him as a stranger; on a rare visit, when she spills a bottle of Coke in his refrigerator, she will be terrified to tell him, having no idea what it looks like when this man gets angry. "Oh, *great*, Lauren," he'll say when she works up the courage. At most four years old, she'll wonder how this news could possibly be great.

The summer before she turns thirteen, when she's just gotten her period for the first time and the father has remarried and had three more children, the daughter will travel to Orange County to visit him and his new family. They'll walk down the hill from his modest gray house to the public beach where surfers bob languidly in the Pacific, the tops of their wetsuits hanging from their waists, waiting patiently for something to happen. In the mornings the father will make bacon and eggs for all four children, scooping cantaloupe with a spoon into smooth little spheres.

One night, when she is supposed to be bunking with her father's twin girls, who are her baby brother's age and fast asleep, she will no longer be able to suppress her panic. She'll picture the surfers, slouching on their gleaming boards, chewing gum and staring at the sky, imagine them feeling it in the water beneath them, that undeniable shift in momentum, the earth telling them, It's time, go.

Planning to use the living room phone to call her mother, to tell her she thinks she might throw up, to beg to come home, the daughter will tiptoe out of the girls' bedroom to find that she is not the only one in the house who is awake.

The father will be in the living room, lying sideways on the couch in front of the television, the volume of some sitcom turned low. He will call her sweetie, he'll ask her what's wrong. He'll give her his place on the couch, make a bed for himself on the floor right in front of her.

When she falls asleep, he will stay right there, on the floor beside her, all night.

At the end of that week, the father will drive her all the way from Orange County to an aunt's house in Las Vegas, where the mother's mother will be waiting to take her home.

But despite the daughter's aching homesickness, her relief at finally being reunited with the grandmother; when the time comes for the father to hug her goodbye, in the aunt's sterile, white-tiled foyer surrounded by the mother's family, the daughter will begin to cry. Her face will come up to the chest of that old turquoise patterned shirt, steeped in cigarette smoke, and she will want to suffocate inside these fumes, not knowing when she will be able to smell them again.

They will stand like this for what feels like a long time, but eventually the father will have to go, it's getting late, he has a long drive back to his home that isn't hers. The turquoise shapes will be soaked through at her eye level. After he's gone, the girl will turn around and see her grandmother crying too. The girl will sob with abandon for hours, at the house, at the Chinese restaurant over dinner, her great aunts and uncles shifting uncomfortably around the lazy Susan. Her grief will embarrass her, but it will refuse to be controlled. It will be the first time she realizes what she's never had.

On January 23, 2023, I learned my unborn daughter would die. That in fact she had been both growing and dying inside of me for weeks, if not months. This would not be the only logical impossibility I'd fail to reconcile from that day on.

My own body was still very much pregnant, ravenous and distended and peeing every fifteen minutes, preparing for new life. But somewhere the less tangible parts of me were already knee-deep in grief, unraveling all the careful plans I'd made in my mind and out loud. Unraveling.

Her "demise," fetal diagnostic specialists in North Carolina and then New York would tell me, was entirely natural, a consequence of pure nature. And yet to me, it has seemed the most unnatural outcome possible: a life ending before it'd even begun.

"It was bad luck," one doctor said, when he confirmed the biopsy results two weeks after her death. Well, sure; but hadn't her very existence been luck too? Had she not also been the luckiest thing to happen to us in our lives?

A little girl died, and then she was born.

. . .

As pieces of my only child are still coming out of me, the single most common phrase I hear from well-meaning doctors, friends, family members, is that I will have another child someday.

I understand why they say these words, feel the love and encouragement in them, know it may even be true. But, I want to ask every one of these people, what if I simply don't? Would all this still be okay then? What if I miss her too much, or I'm tired, or I don't feel like it? What if I can't get pregnant again? What if I do get pregnant and then that baby dies too? What if I'm fairly certain I would not survive that?

Or, best-case scenario, let's imagine that I somehow gather the hope and the herculean patience to do this all over again, to count the weeks and the days and the fruit sizes and the nausea pills and the centimeters, and then, by some miracle, a baby—a second baby—is born. Do you know, I want to ask my sweet cheerleaders of fertility, that even *that* precious gift of a life will not be Simone?

I reach back for my old perspective, the one I had before she was conceived, the one I add to the heaping pile of things I've lost. I'd been so happy, Gabe and I had been so happy, that I'd thought of having children as a nebulous possibility, but not a necessity. I was able to imagine our life together continuing just as we were; felt protective of the time we shared just the two of us.

And yet, I stopped taking birth control after the last day of my period in August. I'd debated this decision for a few months, wanting to get off the hormones I'd been on for a dozen years, wanting my body to recalibrate from the migraines and the distorted periods, to return to some kind of origin state. I did not think, or at least I didn't tell myself, I was trying to get pregnant.

This was, on a more immediate level, because I did not think I could. I'd accidentally devoted my twenties to a vicious eating disorder that considered every food a gastroenterological threat and kept my weight frighteningly low. I survived on a diet of "safe" foods for over a decade: dry crackers and cereals and fruits and English muffins and vegetables, foods I had more or less arbitrarily determined to be safe—or at least less hospitable to bacterial growth than animals and their byproducts. I did not think I had an "eating disorder," because I did not like what was happening to my body on the outside, and I managed just enough self-awareness to be embarrassed by the way that I looked and acted. But I see now that I moved through the world with the disordered eater's trademark hubris: I thought I knew better than everyone else. These poor fools, I thought, ordering their sushi and takeout and aioli and not even asking to what temperature the chicken had been cooked, whether the soft cheese was pasteurized. I alone knew the secrets. I alone was keeping myself safe.

I got better. A few months before my thirtieth birthday I finally conceded to the professional opinion that I take medication. I'd been prescribed SSRIs since I was eighteen, but the anxiety I needed them for also made me too afraid to take them, because of the advertised side effect of nausea.

It was a Saturday in May and I'd woken up alone in my apartment in downtown Manhattan when the dam broke. It wasn't sudden, I'd been feeling the tiny leaks accumulate over the past year, frustrations with the microscopic space I gave myself to live, frustrations that grew into larger ones, which grew into a hunger I hadn't felt in ten years. I held on to the fears as tightly and for as long as I could, believing that if I let them go, the chaos would drown me. I didn't understand at the time that those tiny leaks were the most powerful part of me, my body's will to live.

That morning, as on most mornings when we are apart, my mom called, and she could tell that I was crying. I probably said something mean, maybe I even hung up on her. I couldn't have given you a reason why I was angry at her, except that she has been a bottomless receptacle for my so-called suffering all my life.

Under an hour later there was a knock on my door, and it was Mom, wearing workout pants and sneakers and a baseball hat, which is how you know she left the house in a rush. I don't know why seeing her through the keyhole, standing out there in the drab, gray second-floor elevator landing, her voice calling my name with so much concern, hurt me more than being alone had. Something about feeling unworthy of a love as strong and pure as my mother's.

We walked on the West Side Highway and I continued to be a huge bitch, in the way a four-year-old behaves when she's overtired. Craving my mother's attention and then dismissing it when it arrived, bristling against the care I wasn't able to give back to her or to anyone or myself.

I don't remember when she left, or when I called Devin, my

best friend who would later become Simone's godmother, but I remember that she came over without hesitation, a bottle of wine in her large black handbag, and sat with me on the couch as I opened the untouched pill bottle, took one, and then waited for something bad to happen. Meanwhile, Devin put on *Big Brother*, a show she loved and always wanted me to also love. She snort-laughed at the low-budget sound effects and the slapstick comedy of bodies being dunked and slimed, and I laughed at her snort-laughs. At some point that night I felt safe and tired enough to fall asleep.

Ten days later, over Memorial Day weekend, when I met Devin and our brothers at a carnival in Asbury Park, I told her I hadn't pooped since that first pill, a Lexapro. It was kind of the opposite of throwing up, I said as we went higher and higher on a Ferris wheel, the wind blowing our hair in wild directions, so strong up there I had to yell so she could hear me. I found the whole situation uncomfortable and very funny. I switched to Zoloft, checked myself into an eight-week outpatient eating disorder treatment program, and the rest is history. After a long battle with my broken brain, my body won.

In the meantime, it was not lost on me that I hadn't gotten my period from the ages of twenty to thirty-one. Like every bodily function, ovulation and menstruation require calories to burn, and these are among the first processes the body compromises when it detects the need to conserve—when it is starving. I'd gotten my health back, my self back; I didn't think to ask for more.

Then I met Gabe. In December 2019, I'd received at my office one of the many books it is my job to consider for a review. This one, a novel, was a bright, taxi yellow, and I began to read it at my desk. There is no rhyme or reason to how long my colleagues and I spend with books we're considering; maybe I'll skim the whole thing if it's nonfiction, or if it's debut fiction I'll read the first fifty or one hundred pages, hoping to get a better feel for the voice.

This taxi-yellow book, though, I finished. Right at my desk. I didn't mean to, it just happened. I will not tell you that I fell in love with its author right then, because I didn't. I will only tell you that young Claude, his grandmother, his girlfriend, and the old man crying under the bed made me feel a depth of emotion only the most human characters can. Knowing nothing of this writer, I admired and respected him. He also made me laugh a lot. I assigned the book for a review.

This happened in the morning, on a Friday in early December. It was the birthday of my coworker Tas, a close friend. To celebrate we took tiny edibles in the back stairwell and went to Schnipper's for lunch. In the elevator back up to the office, we ran into the head of the newspaper's culture desk. I suddenly panicked that I was too high (I was objectively not high at all), and that he could tell, and that he would tell my boss and/or everyone. Then he was asking me a question. Was I reading anything good? Okay. You got this. You can answer this one. I told him I had just finished a book in one sitting at my desk. That its cover was taxi yellow. I could not for the life of me remember what it was called.

When I got back to my desk, I emailed the culture editor the title and author of this book. He thanked me. I don't know if he ever read it. Three years later, this editor is my boss, and this author is my husband.

When the review of the yellow book ran, the author followed me on Twitter. I followed him back. Through some innocuous, bare-minimum internet research, the desk's fact-checker, Lovia—also my good friend—helped me determine that the author lived in Buffalo. Oh well.

For the next year, the first year of COVID, our ensuing correspondence was entirely professional. I edited his review of another novel. My then boss let me know when the yellow book won a prize; I congratulated the author. We both had relationships with other people.

By December 2020, I was living alone in a rented house at the base of Franklin Hills, in the Los Feliz neighborhood of Los Angeles. I'd moved out there on a whim, because I'd always wanted to and because the office was no longer an option—and because for the first time in my life, I wasn't afraid to leave my mother. Maybe it was because COVID had grounded her from all travel and I'd finally felt her presence as something reliable and certain, or maybe the Zoloft was really kicking in. But I finally felt ready to move away.

Also for the first time, I started seeing my father almost weekly out in California. He'd drive two hours from his apartment in Carlsbad or I'd drive down there and we'd order pizza and talk about our lives. He was leaving his job running a network of nursing homes, and his parents were moving from Irvine to Montana. His siblings—he grew up the oldest of eleven—had persuaded their dad to buy a dude ranch as their new home, for the entire Christensen clan to enjoy. With hundreds of grand-children and great-grandchildren, the family could descend on Grammy and Grandad's with the might of a full summer camp. The house, my dad said, would have ATVs and a zip line.

I lied and said that sounded fun. He said it wasn't; he was wor-ried about his parents, both in their eighties and declining in health. My dad worried this move would kill them.

It was strange to see the parts of myself I'd gotten from my dad even though he didn't raise me. People who don't really know us say that I am just like my mom—we look similar, and have the same voice, and wear the same size clothes and shoes. But outside of work, my mom is reserved, reticent, a listener; at a certain point in any social interaction, I can feel her go quiet, sense her need to detach, to be alone. Both my father and I, I learned in my thirties, were sharers, elaborators; we never got tired of the sound of our own voices.

At some point during the year I was living there, after a very sporadic chain of work-related email correspondences, I received a perfectly chaste and friendly message from Gabe that nonethe-less gave me subtle reason to wonder if he was still dating his girlfriend. I sent a screenshot to Lovia. She texted back: "Are you going to have sex with Gabriel Bump?"

A couple of months and many FaceTimes later, I drove to pick him up at LAX. No one our age was vaccinated yet, so our first date involved ten days, four brain swabs, a day trip to an outdoor bookstore in Ojai, and a lot of takeout. I learned that he spoke so softly you sometimes couldn't hear him, and that he walked on his tiptoes, a lifelong habit, something about his high arches and childhood casts that didn't work. He was so gentle that when he found out my beagle, Q, slept in a crate in another room, he couldn't handle it; on the first night we met he began a "Free Q" campaign, and she's slept in bed with us ever since.

By the next year, we'd bought a house together in Chapel Hill, North Carolina, where he was in his second semester teaching creative writing at UNC. I'd left LA but had gotten permission to continue working remotely for the time being. The decision was big, but never uncertain. We were starting to build a life together.

That life did not, in my mind then, necessarily include a baby. I didn't understand what people meant when they said they "wanted children"—just abstractly, just anyone? Of course I could wrap my head around a parent's specific love for a specific child, but just amorphously pining for a human being who didn't exist yet, knowing only that they'd be yours? In the absence of such a concrete love, a life with Gabe alone seemed to me as full as a life could possibly be.

I have heard that my aunt Michelle is convinced, I guess timing-wise, that Simone was conceived at her beach house in Santa Cruz, which Gabe and I borrowed for a few days in August. The truth is although I was no longer on birth control on that road trip down the California coast, I'd barely let Gabe touch me since he'd gotten food poisoning several days before, on the drive from Healdsburg to San Francisco. I hadn't been sure it was food poisoning, and was scared he might have had something contagious, so on this would-be romantic vacation I avoided contact with him as much as I could. Even days after he'd recovered, I slept separately from him and would only let him hug me from behind, so his spit droplets were less likely to make their way to my mouth.

We probably had sex at some point that month, but I have no idea if I was ovulating, and my period arrived on September 2, back home in Chapel Hill, in the half bathroom under the stairs. My disappointment floored me. I hadn't known how I'd felt about my own potential motherhood until that moment, and when I told Gabe, he said that was okay, we'd try again. I hadn't realized we'd been trying, but now I did. Maybe I'd hoped to avoid disappointment by carving out an imaginary in-between state of passivity where I wasn't actively warding off pregnancy, but neither was I taking deliberate steps toward it, not even counting days to determine when I was ovulating. (My therapist saw it differently: If I was neither menopausal nor using any form of birth control, she said, then I was trying to become pregnant.)

At around two a.m. on September 14, my grandmother's ninetieth birthday, Gabe's fifteen-year-old cat, Hootie, died in his arms in our bed. She'd been sick for a week, her kidneys failing, barely eating or drinking, her small body high on painkillers that made her wander around in circles, bumping into walls, trying to walk up them like a ladder. Gabe spent the entire week holding her, driving her back and forth to vets in Durham and Winston-Salem, bringing his Bible in the passenger seat of his car. That night, as Q and I slept beside them, Hootie's body went stiff in Gabe's arms, and then he felt her every muscle relax, the wetness of her urine on the sheets. We have her paw print in some kind of sand that someone at the animal hospital took in the middle of the night, after they'd confirmed her gone.

The next day, still red-eyed from crying, I made myself take Q on a walk around the neighborhood, and we ran into a gangly black-and-white puppy on Franklin Street. I stopped because Q wanted to play with him, even brought him a little stick she found to play with together, and I told the woman walking him what a sweet puppy she had.

She was just fostering him, she said. He'd been found in a box on the side of the road in Durham, the whole litter named after music festivals in the South. His name, she said, was Hopscotch. Did I know of anyone who was looking to adopt a puppy?

I called Gabe, certain he'd tell me it was too soon. "It's a sign from Hoot," he said instead. "She's telling us it's okay to move on." I sat on someone's uneven stone wall and filled out an application on the shelter's website on my phone.

I can't remember what days we had sex that month, but I know that a couple weeks after my period I left for New York, to celebrate my mom's birthday on the eighteenth, and stayed there for a week. My brother, Jamie, and I made dinner for Mom and lost the 4 candle somewhere in Whole Foods, so the cake just had a 6 on it. Another night that week, I went to a coworker's retirement party on the Upper West Side, and afterward a late, boozy dinner at a French restaurant nearby; I called Gabe to gossip about it on the way home.

I spent my last day in New York at home alone with my grandfather, my Gong Gong, who'd moved with my grandmother, Poh Poh, from their home of sixty years in Wellesley, Massachusetts, into my mom's New York apartment during the pandemic. He was ninety-four and his Parkinson's and dementia had been steadily worsening for the past few years. To curb the downward progression, he now had to take two pills three times a day: at nine a.m., three p.m., and nine p.m. This regimen occupied and confused him greatly. He would sit at the kitchen table staring at his phone for hours, waiting for the alarm to tell him it was time to take the next dose. We asked: Did he need to use the bathroom? Did he want to watch TV? Was he hungry? "No, two forty-two," he'd tell us, pointing to the clock on his touchscreen. "Eighteen minutes."

That day, my mom was at a meeting and my grandmother was spending the night at an orthopedic rehab facility after hip surgery, and I was sitting across from Gong Gong at the kitchen table where he spent most of his waking hours, working on my laptop while he played solitaire. Sometimes, when he "got stuck" or the game was "no good," we'd have to gently help him along, as he didn't always notice when there was a move to make.

He must have felt restless, or thought I was being boring, because he asked me if I wanted to go for a walk. He'd become so inert and passive by then that someone else always had to coax him into doing things—taking a shower, going for a walk, eating a meal, watching TV. For him to suggest an activity felt unusual. I think now that it may have been something he wanted to do just with me.

I got his walker and put his cell phone (an old iPhone of my mom's that had a yellow Post-it taped to the back of it that said "9AM 3PM 9PM / ANDREA 917-XXX-XXXX / LENA 781-XXX-XXXX" in big bold letters) in his pocket, because he liked to keep track of his steps. There was some app that someone had configured so that when he hit a thousand in one day, the bar turned green. "I'm green today" was a common refrain when he'd done several circles around the kitchen island, as was a disappointed "today's orange" when he'd felt too tired or been too busy with doctors' appointments to spend hours pacing the apartment with his walker.

Outside, we took slow steps and he told me the direction Mom always took him in. First we turned left outside our build-ing, walking east down the street until we reached the syna-gogue, where two security officers said hello to us like they knew him. Then we turned around at Lex and reached Park again and turned right, heading north. At the next corner there was a blue mailbox that he called the post office. We turned right again onto a busy two-way street and walked toward a party supply store in the middle of the block where a few bal-loons were always tied outside. "We walk to the bubbles and then turn around," he told me, his happiness as plain and pure as a child's.

That night, after I'd ordered us Chinese takeout and the clock slowly approached nine p.m., he became particularly agitated about the pill schedule. He confided to me that "they"—I fig-ured he meant my mom and grandmother—had lately been "fouling up" his doses, the quantities and times changing on him in disorienting ways.

Sitting next to him at the kitchen table, I found a loose sheet of paper and drew a single line on it, representing a twenty-four-hour period. I used little ticks to mark twelve a.m. and noon and the next twelve a.m., and then bigger ticks to denote the times he was meant to take the pills. I was trying to comfort him, re-ground him in a sense of linear time, but this no longer meant anything to Gong Gong. Though he concentrated very hard, fussing the piece of paper in his hands and furrowing his bushy gray eyebrows, his confusion persisted. The only thing left to do when this happened—and it would happen again and again, with increasing agitation and severity, for the few months he had left—was to change the subject.

The kitchen chair he sat in faced a pale gray wall with a painting on it. It's a painting my mom has had for years, an abstract black outline of three people, two men and one woman, standing with either three regular bicycles or maybe one regular and one tandem bicycle; it's ambiguous. Gong Gong must have spent, in his lifetime, what amounted to full weeks looking at this painting, sitting in that seat, eating breakfast, napping, eating lunch and dinner, waiting for his pills. Tonight, he told me the painting was moving.

"Now I see six people," he said after counting each one under his breath in Cantonese. A minute later: "Now there are no people at all; just seven chairs."

I asked him if he felt upset about these visions, and he shook his head. "It's very strange," he said, shaking his head like he was the only person in the world who could see it for what it was. "I wonder if Andrea knows that this painter painted multiple pictures. A moving picture."

That night when it came time to give him his nine p.m. pills, I discovered more than just the two Parkinson's pills left in the little Saturday compartment of the plastic pillbox he obsessively opened and closed all day long, prompting Poh Poh to screech that he was going to break it.

I wasn't sure what those extra pills were for, or if I should give them to him, since clearly these were meant to be taken on Saturday. What if he'd already taken the Saturday pills and then someone had refilled them, or he'd taken pills from another day instead of Saturday? I didn't want to overdose him; but what if he had just forgotten to take these, and I let him go a day without meds he needed?

Panicking, I called my mom, who didn't answer, and then I called my grandmother. She told me to calm down. Those other pills were for some other things, maybe his prostate, maybe his memory; anyway they didn't really matter, she said. Just give them to him, he'll be fine.

I did give him the pills, and remained vigilant for signs of overdose, even though I had no idea what those would even be. I couldn't bear to leave him alone, so when he got into bed I asked if I could get in the large bed with him, on Poh Poh's side, and watch TV until Mom got home. He looked surprised, but also pleased. "Okay," he said, in the cheerful, singsongy lilt with which he agreed to most things you presented to him. He was smiling his big smile.

He had already changed into his pajamas, brushed his teeth, and cleaned his face, and now spent several minutes compulsively smoothing out the large disposable pad he slept on top of every night, in case he had an accident. His long, thin fingers looked so delicate, almost feminine, as they pulled taut the corners and edges, making sure it was all just right.

It seemed to me that he began snoring before he was horizontal. I cannot remember what I put on the TV, only that I felt comforted by the smell of him, of his plaid long-sleeved pajamas, that smell I remembered from my childhood, when I'd run into the bedroom he shared with my grandmother in Wellesley and jump on their bed.

"Say, 'Gong Gong, zao,'" she'd call out to me from the bathroom, standing at the mirror in her silk pajamas, putting on lotion or blow-drying her hair. I'd repeat after her, Mandarin for good morning, and he'd respond, "Guai Guai, zao." This is what he always called me (when he wasn't accidentally calling me Andrea), a term of endearment, kind of like sweetheart. He'd be at the sink next to hers, running an electric razor over his chin and neck and cheeks; or maybe stretching in front of the bed while watching the local morning news, hands on his hips, moving them in big circles clockwise and then counterclockwise. I'd laugh at the movements and ask what he was doing. "Try it," he'd say, and we'd do them next to each other, two hula-hoopers in slow motion.

Twenty-six years later, that house he built long since sold to another, younger family, his body so much weaker and mine so much stronger, I lay next to him and watched the light from the TV make different shadows on his face. I watched his wild gray eyebrows rise and fall as he dreamt whatever he was dreaming, probably in Cantonese. As his dementia had advanced in recent years, he'd started retreating more and more back to his first language, forgetting the English words he'd spoken for seventy-something years living in Canada and America, remembering only the ones his brain had learned as a boy, the youngest of three in his family, left behind in Hong Kong by his parents and older brothers, who'd moved to Toronto intending for him to later follow, when the Japanese occupied his home city, Kowloon, leaving him to support himself and his aging grandmother, her feet bound. He was only thirteen.

Eighty-one years later, he slept peacefully in a spacious bedroom in his daughter's home, the room that was once my brother's, dark blue and white and covered in Legos, now an elegant pale gray and decorated with Gong Gong's old midcentury walnut furniture and framed scrolls bearing his own trained calligraphy. Mom came home, and I heard her look for me in my room, in the kitchen, in the TV room, unsure where I could possibly be. She found me in Gong Gong's bed and assured me everything was fine. I kissed his forehead, left his room, and went to mine.

Mom talked a lot about his dignity in the twilight of his life—how difficult it was for my grandfather to let her clean him up when he lost control of his bowel movements, one of his earliest muscles to succumb to the Parkinson's. "He's always been so dignified," she'd say. "It kills me to see him ashamed."

But this always sounded wrong to me. The human body isn't supposed to be dignified. I'd remind her and my grandmother over and over: That time when I threw up in his bathroom sink in the middle of the night when I was six, because I couldn't make it to the toilet, and I was so afraid and thought I was dying, did he make me feel undignified? Did he think my body was gross because I could not control it? No, he let me finish, rubbed my back, and cleaned it up. At two a.m., he let me take his spot in the bed and fall asleep next to my grandmother while he spent the rest of the night scrubbing my vomit out of the porcelain.

I wanted him to know that his body was just like everyone else's, miraculous and embarrassing, fundamentally ungovernable. That despite our delusions, when it came down to it, none of us ever had much control over our lives, or our deaths, at all.

I came back to North Carolina. Gabe and I had a supervised visit with Hopscotch, the woman who was fostering him, and a representative from the shelter on an empty baseball field at a local park. It was sunset, and the air was starting to smell the slightest bit like fall. His foster mother told us she and her children had been calling him Steve. He and Q zoomed in wide, concentric circles around the field, their bodies then around the same height and length, though Q was thicker around the middle, shorter-legged but in immense control of her movements; the puppy awkward, gangly and desperate in his. They took turns humping each other, which was funny when it was Q's turn on top because that's not actually how that works.

When this puppy joined our family, on the afternoon of Wednesday, September 27, we kept his original name. The following Saturday, when my period was only one day late, I took Hopscotch to his first puppy training class, where I trailed him for 120 minutes straight, feeding him a constant stream of kibble and treats as he played in tunnels and obstacle courses with the other puppies. When our puppies weren't behaving correctly, the class leader, a middle-aged woman with pigtails, would slip us "higher value" treats, pieces of string cheese and nubs of cold, slippery hot dog.

Back at home, Hop and I both passed out next to Gabe on the couch, my arms around Hop as we both snored. When I woke up, Gabe and I both remarked that it was unusual for me to nap at all. In fact I hated napping, even when I had jet lag—it reminded me of being sick. It must be the exhaustion from having a new puppy, we said.

When my period was two days late, a major thunderstorm knocked out the power in our neighborhood. Gabe and I were both overwhelmed with Hop and Q trapped inside, and I continued to feel exhausted. At one point the dogs were freaking out over the same toy, and their fight spiraled into one between Gabe and me. I—erratically, stupidly—got both dogs in the car, thinking I could take them to a friend's house who had power. The rain was so heavy that I pulled over in a strip-mall parking lot near our house, outside the steak restaurant Gabe and I had gone to for his birthday a few months earlier. I wept in the car, dramatically and for no real reason that I could discern. Gabe called several times asking me to come home, he was worried, it wasn't safe on the roads. I did. Our power came back on, and the house and I calmed down.

The next morning at 5:36 a.m., I texted my mom, "Three days late. Should I take test?" She'd just landed in London for a board meeting. The company was hiring a new CEO, and she was leading the search committee. She told me not to be nervous. She suggested I wait until I was a week late.

I didn't wait. I'd "casually" bought a pack of three tests the last time I'd been at Target, just to have them now that I wasn't on birth control anymore. I peed on one and immediately saw two dark pink lines. My heart raced, and I laughed nervously, alone in the bathroom, my feet cold on the gray tiled floor. The magnitude of that moment, the disbelief, the abject panic, the humility. I knew in that second I was powerless, and would follow this flicker of a being wherever she took me, for the rest of my life.

I got back into bed. Gabe was still asleep. I said, loudly, "Gabe," and he jolted awake, asking what was wrong. He later said that I held both of my cheeks as I told him. Maybe it was to keep my head from spinning off my body. "I'm pregnant." He closed his eyes and smiled a smile I will never forget—as blissful and calm as if he'd known all along. I was crying and laughing, struggling to control my breathing, my heart racing. "I'm going to be so sick," I said, but in that moment I knew I'd handle it, whatever came. Q came up from under the covers to lick our tears. Then she saw it was still dark out and went back to sleep.

I called Mom, who was just getting to her hotel. She yelled, "What?" She yelled about being a grandmother. She yelled, "How am I supposed to focus in this meeting at all now?"

The box had two more tests, and I took those also. The dark second lines showed up right away.

I told a few more people that day—my cousins, Liz and Caroline, who are like my sisters; Devin; Lovia; Kate, my friend from college who'd happened to move to North Carolina just before I did, so we now lived less than thirty minutes apart. I knew you weren't supposed to tell people before twelve weeks, but that seemed insanely far away and I also knew, even then, that if I lost the pregnancy, a not insignificant possibility that early on, there was no way I was going through that alone.

Liz picked up first, even though she lives in San Francisco and it was early in the morning. "Was this planned?" she asked, and then apologized seven hundred times afterward for asking that, even though I felt the question to be extremely fair. Liz was born less than two years after me, and we look so alike people often mistake us for sisters. She's always been infinitely more rational, organized, intentional about her life than I am, in a way that makes me regard her like the older sister, a steady guide. She'd gotten married that February, to an equally intentional, rigorously moral and intelligent man named Sam, and I knew they were taking the question of their own family planning seriously. Whatever secondhand anxiety she felt at this surprise news was far overshadowed by joy, and love.

We'd been so close all our lives that her directness didn't faze me; also the idea of an "unplanned pregnancy" made me feel young. But just because we didn't check when I was ovulating or do IVF does not mean this pregnancy was unwanted. From the first second we knew about her, Simone brought Gabe and me to our knees. I said some version of this to Liz. My feeling was that there is only so much you can really, truly plan for in life— what job to apply for, where you'd like to live, what you're going to do for dinner. Nature felt too powerful to fuck with, so I'd felt afraid to try.

Liz and her younger sister, Caroline, grew up in the Bay Area, while Jamie and I were in New York; but our small family made a point to spend most holidays together, and every summer (when

Jamie was either not born yet or too little to join us) the three girls would meet at Poh Poh and Gong Gong's house in Welles-ley to go to a day camp there for a few weeks. We slept in my uncle's old bedroom, which was big enough for one twin bed and my grandfather's drafting table, but when we arrived with our screaming and our cranberry-apple juice he moved his of-fice somewhere else so we could squeeze a cot and an air mat-tress into the tiniest bedroom in the house and all sleep together. We always said we'd rotate who got the bed, but I always ended up with it.

Liz and Caroline fought over me in those days, making me sit in between them at the breakfast table and in the middle seat of the car; following me around Gap Kids, picking up every shirt I picked up and then putting it back when I did; dutifully execut-ing every weird scheme I came up with, including making a play on our grandparents' deck about a dog, a cat, and a mouse. To come outside and see it, we made our grandparents buy ticket stubs from a large roll they'd bought for us at Staples.

Right away, Caroline said she hoped I was having a girl. "Then we'd have four generations of women in our family," she said: Poh Poh, Mom, me, and the baby. I said girls were too hard, I wanted a boy. Admitting that kills me now, because I didn't even mean it, and because I fear I somehow wished her away. Really, I was over the moon to be having a girl. The boy thing is just a holdover from my own upbringing: Between my brother and me, there was no contest over who has made Mom's life more difficult.

Caroline had just finished business school and moved to Williamsburg with her longtime boyfriend, Sebastian, a tall, self-possessed German man whose authenticity and sense of humor put everyone around him at ease. After like a decade of dating Caroline he's as much a part of our family as she is. They were in an Airbnb at the time, trying to find a more permanent rental, and they'd end up hopping from one short-term deal to another for months, booking things and packing up at the eleventh hour in a way that exemplified both New York reality and their shared resistance to logistical panic. They love each other in a way that needs no explanation or timeline, and I respect their unbothered approach to the world's nosy questions about marriage and children. Sebastian has two young nieces in the town near Frankfurt where his parents and sister still live, and Caroline dotes on them, learning German to keep up with theirs, buying them matching floral-print outfits and little pink suitcases, and sending us pictures and videos of them constantly.

I felt my heart physically expanding as I listened to her prepare in her mind for this tiny niece, long before she was born. Caroline would come down from New York and babysit all the time, she said. She had me send her pictures of the bedroom where the nursery would go—currently Hopscotch's bedroom, where the shelter had persuaded Gabe to keep him in a large crate—so she could start pulling ideas for how to decorate it.

I told Jamie by sending him a link to a T-shirt that said NACHO AVERAGE UNCLE on it with a drawing of three chips covered in cheese. He responded, "lol this cannot be how this info is conveyed to me."

I FaceTimed my grandparents, who'd just moved into an assisted living facility seven blocks from my mom's apartment in

New York. They were sitting on the couch in their sitting room, and Poh Poh told Gong Gong, "Look, it's Lauren!"

I said I was pregnant, due in June, they were going to be great-grandparents. Poh Poh was excited, but distracted with making sure my grandfather was sitting squarely in the frame, making sure he understood.

As usual, he was smiling his big, open-mouthed smile, and I wasn't sure he knew what was going on. But then he said, "Good news." He said, "How many months?" I didn't know then that it would be the last time I spoke to him when he was conscious. I will never, ever forget his joy.

My grandmother, unsurprisingly, asked if we were going to get married. I told her we were.

Gabe and I had known we'd be married eventually, but until Simone we'd felt no urgency; we'd signed a thirty-year mortgage together, and every other kind of commitment felt kind of decorative. Except, obviously, a child.

Sometime that week, that first week we knew about Simone, I was working from home and Gabe went out to run errands; I asked him to pick me up a burrito. When he got back, I was on my laptop at the kitchen table. He handed me the burrito wrapped in warm tinfoil and I immediately started unwrapping it. By the time I'd taken the first bite, he was on his knee, holding a clam-shell jewelry box with a yellow diamond necklace inside. He asked me to marry him, even though we'd already decided we would. I hugged him and cried, my mouth still full of chorizo.

What I'd really wanted, before Simone, was to elope, to tell our vows to each other and no one else, quietly, like we would on any other day. A large wedding felt so intimidating to me—not so much the stress of planning it as the pressure of enduring it. What if I asked a hundred people to come see me walk down some aisle and then, when that moment came, I had to throw up? Or wanted to be alone and cry, or just wanted to go home?

Simone changed the calculus in every way, including this one. Now, we were not just performing our existing love with a party, but honoring a whole new life, one who existed within but also outside of us. We were celebrating the joining of our two families in a way that was not just symbolic, but real, embodied.

Also, given the enormity of what was about to happen in our lives, planning a small wedding felt chill and fun, inconsequential.

We decided on a ceremony in early December, when I'd be thirteen weeks pregnant. Gabe's father, Tom, would officiate in my mom's living room in New York, the home I'd lived in since I was twelve. Only our closest family members would be there: our parents and my grandparents; Gabe's older sister, Natalie, and his older brother, Mike; Jamie; Liz and Caroline; my uncle Mark and Gabe's aunt Jo. Gabe's three-year-old nephew, Baldwin, would be our flower boy; even my father would be driving across the country to be there. We'd all have dinner around one big table in the dining room, and if I felt nauseous or tired or if Baldwin had a tantrum or if my grandfather had an accident, no problem, we'd just be at home.

As it turned out, of course, Mom was left to plan the whole thing, as the next two months felled me. Some days I was so nauseous that I thought multiple times I might also have a stomach virus. If I went more than an hour without eating, I would be on the verge of vomiting. For all of October and November I subsisted on a near-constant stream of buttered toast and soup crackers and apple juice with a lot of ice, instant ramen if I could handle it.

Due to my lifelong emetophobia, I almost always have a bottle of the prescription antiemetic Zofran on me. I've taken it less than a handful of times in the past decade, but carry it with me always—a kind of security blanket. Unfortunately, this drug now proved totally ineffective. Instead, I got a prescription for a combination of vitamin B6 and doxylamine, which did work, but I suspect only by completely knocking me out. If I got nauseous at ten a.m. on a Wednesday, when I was meant to be working, I would have to try to push through it until it was late enough in the day that I could take the medication and fall into a bottomless and unyielding sleep.

Which, by the way, I did not need help with. Throughout my pregnancy, sleep came mightily and of its own volition. At seven p.m., or two a.m., or ten a.m., even after I'd slept eleven hours the night before. I could fall asleep anywhere, with anyone in the room, midsentence. And there was none of my usual fitful, half-awake tossing or four a.m. wakefulness: My body sucked down sleep greedily, urgently; when I became tired, sleep was no longer optional.

From the earliest days, pregnancy struck me as a profound distillation of physical need: Things like sleep and food and water were no longer optional cravings I could put off until after a meeting, or when I got home, until a later time that would be more convenient. Working remotely from home, I fortunately could fall asleep for up to three hours in the middle of a workday without anyone seeing me, because when I felt the need to sleep, there was no stopping it. Ditto having to pee. My eating adhered not to structured meals but violent impulses, my hunger no longer a suggestion but an emergency. Whatever Simone needed, I had to give her.

At eight and a half weeks, I went to the emergency room. It was a Tuesday night in November, and we were in bed watching TV when I started to feel cramps. Growing up, I'd had only a handful of painful periods, and for most of my adulthood I'd not had a period at all. All to say, this pain seemed to me out of the ordinary and extreme.

We called Gabe's mom, Debbie, a nurse and former doula in Chicago. She said my uterus was growing, and that hurts. An hour later it had gotten worse, and I left a message for the obstetrician on call at my practice. Gabe insisted on calling Debbie this time; I hadn't wanted to bother her again. "Just go to the emergency room," she told him. "Better safe than sorry." My OB called back and confirmed: Since I hadn't yet had any ultrasound at all, they needed to rule out an ectopic pregnancy. I'd need to confirm that this pregnancy was in my uterus, and not in one of my fallopian tubes—a condition that would be fatal for the baby and could be for me as well.

We sat in the ER waiting area at UNC for hours, amid families and couples and a group of college boys watching *Game of Thrones* on a laptop ("Khaleesi is way less hot in real life," a skinny boy in shorts and dirty sneakers told his friends) and coughs and blood-soaked bandages and more than one person asleep and surrounded by what seemed like all their worldly possessions. We ate granola bars and drank Sprite from the vending machine, played Words with Friends. I held my regular-sized belly instinctively, in both pain and pride; I wasn't here for myself, I was subconsciously indicating. I'm here for my child.

When my name was finally called, I was escorted down so many hallways to the maternal health wing, where a young, blond sonographer denied my request to have Gabe in the room with me. Since my pregnancy was so early, she explained, she had to use the more invasive transvaginal ultrasound, as opposed to the external transabdominal one. As she stuck the device inside me and moved it around for what turned out to be forty minutes, I tried to focus on the small television screen to my right, which was playing *Below Deck* on mute. In this episode, one of the crewmembers had food poisoning, and the rest of her coworkers were pissed that she wasn't able to help them cater to their drunk patrons. I tried to read the blank expression of the technician's eyes above her mask as she clicked away on the keyboard.

When I could no longer stand not knowing, I asked the sonographer what she saw. She couldn't tell me, she said; she'd have to give all her findings to the doctor, who would take a look and explain everything to me.

"Tonight?" I asked.

"Yes, hopefully in a couple of hours," she said.

The only other time we spoke was when she explained that the reason she was prodding so forcefully to my left was because she was having trouble seeing my left ovary.

"There's a lot of gas blocking it," she told me without emotion. A few minutes later, she found the ovary. "The gas," she said, "it's cleared up." I texted this sequence of events to the group chat I have with five friends from college, and because it was after one a.m. by now, only Emily, who lives in Abu Dhabi, was awake. "I object to the fact that farts can be visible," she said.

After the technician had finished and left the room to let me get dressed, I noticed the images she'd taken were left up on the screen. I wonder to this day if she left them on purpose, a small little rebellion against a system that forbade her from putting a mother's mind at ease at one in the morning. It was a grid of maybe twenty images, labeled with terms I could not interpret. UTERUS TRANS. YS. RT ADNEXA LONG TRANS. I took a picture of the screen and showed Gabe back out in the waiting room as we awaited the doctor. I tried googling what healthy eight-week sonograms were supposed to look like, but the internet wasn't very helpful. To my naked eye the tiny figures seemed to show a fetus in a uterus, but I knew too little about my own anatomy (what does a fallopian tube look like on a sonogram?) to get my hopes up.

Sometime after two a.m., a male doctor pulled back the curtain of our little section in the triage center and confirmed the pregnancy was not ectopic, that the baby was right where it should be. Our expressions of relief must have tipped him off. The doctor said, "Wait, is this your first sonogram?" We told him it was, and he excitedly left to go get a machine to show us himself. That night, surrounded by the sounds and smells of illness and pain, Gabe and I heard our child's heartbeat for the first time, fast and strong. Gabe started to cry. The doctor told us that if you listen to an adult's heartbeat, it doesn't sound all that different. On the short drive home, we imagined that we'd been the best thing to happen to this ER doctor all night.

A little over a week later, we went to my ob-gyn for another, official ultrasound. This time, a kind older woman with a thick Carolina accent performed the scan using a wand over my belly. We saw the baby resting at the bottom of my uterus, a tiny torso flanked by bent, spidery limbs and an egg-shaped head. The technician moved the wand and turned on the sound so we could hear the heartbeat again. Again, Gabe began to cry. "Best sound in the world, isn't it?" the sonographer said. We agreed it was.

Gabe asked if we could take home a picture of our child, and when she moved the wand again to take a screen grab the most incredible thing happened—the baby was now moving. I would imitate that movement for everyone I saw for days, weeks, months afterward: nodding my head exaggeratedly forward and back, pumping my bent arms in a frantic approximation of waving. "He's saying hi to us," I said. (I'm not sure why I'd been so sure she was a boy—maybe because she was bald? I'd talked about naming the baby Max, the name my mom had given the son she lost before I was born. Now, I think, I brought this bad luck upon us.)

As we were being shuttled from that ultrasound room into a regular exam room to meet the midwife, the sonographer bid us goodbye. "It's wonderful to see such happiness," she said. "Y'all are going to be great parents."

A midwife, A, whom we would come to know rather intimately over the next few months, entered the exam room. I felt safe with her immediately: She was articulate and matter-of-fact, but still warm and empathetic. "I've looked at the scans and charts and this is exactly what I want to see at ten weeks," she said. I felt like I'd aced a test, though of course I hadn't done anything to deserve the grade. My body was handling everything on its own; all I had to do was let it.

She asked if we'd thought about genetic testing. I was thirty-three, and without any other risk factors she said they didn't start recommending it until a patient was thirty-five—a cutoff that felt so arbitrary to me every time I heard it—but if we were people who wanted more information rather than less, noninvasive prenatal testing could screen the baby for signs of chromosomal abnormality. It's not as certain as an amniocentesis, she said, but nor does it involve a needle pierced directly into the amniotic sac, which presents a small risk of miscarriage. If the NIPT came back with positive indicators for anything, like Down syndrome or trisomy 13, we could then decide whether to do an amnio to confirm. I told the midwife I wanted to do the test, I wanted to know everything I could know as soon as I could know it. "I've never been one to revel in uncertainty," I said, and gave the requisite blood.

That weekend Lovia came down to visit, made us a gorgeous Spanish omelet and a buttermilk roast chicken, and let me whine at her about not feeling well the entire time. We got manicures and I copied the color she was getting, and then I insisted on driving to Durham for a specific burger and ice cream, but by the time we got there, all I could have was bread and three ginger ales.

A week later, I spent a sunny Saturday afternoon with Kate and her family in Durham. We met at a busy café near their house, but when we got there the line was too long to wait for a table. We put in a take-out order—breakfast sandwiches and fancy salads and a quiche-of-the-day for Kate's eighteen-month-old daughter, Georgia—and went back to their house to wait for it. I'd brought my own emergency crackers to tide me over, and Georgia reached out her hand for some, eating one or two and shuffling over the rest to her mom and dad.

When I got in my car to drive home, I had several missed calls and texts from Gabe, asking if I was okay. Only when I called him back did I realize why: We'd ended up eating lunch an hour after I'd thought we would, and I had completely forgotten an entire plan that we'd made to attend our friends' poetry reading. It wasn't the end of the world, but it shocked me, and it made Gabe worry because of how rarely I even show up late to something, let alone forget about it altogether.

Now we were each driving home, the donut I bought for him at the café sitting next to me in the passenger seat. There was a football game that afternoon, and so traffic was horrific trying to get through campus to our house. I saw families taking pictures together at iconic spots on campus. Small children trailing behind mothers, annoying and happy. The stop-and-go made me nauseous, and to curb it I took small bites of Gabe's donut.

When I got home, I took Q out to pee and then checked my email on the living room couch. The results of my genetic screening had come in. I called Gabe, still in the same traffic but close to home. I can still feel the adrenaline of that moment.

"I don't know if I can wait for you to open this," I said.

"I know," he said. "You can open it, I'll be home soon."

Next to the list of chromosomal abnormalities on the left— TRISOMY 21 (DOWN SYNDROME), TRISOMY 18 (EDWARDS SYNDROME), TRISOMY 13 (PATAU SYNDROME)—every result read "Negative." Below, next to FETAL SEX, it read "Consistent with Female."

I stopped reading. I thought this test told me there was nothing wrong with her chromosomal makeup. I did not read the detailed print below, next to a section that said TEST METHOD. I did not read where it said:

> Optional findings based on the test order include sex chromosome aneuploidy (SCA) [2], and enhanced sequencing series (ESS) [3], which will only be reported on as an additional finding when an abnormality is detected. SCA testing includes information on X and Y representation, while ESS testing includes deletions in selected regions (22q, 15q, 11q, 8q, 5p, 4p, 1p) and trisomy of chromosomes 16 and 22.

I did not read further down, next to a section called PERFOR-
MANCE CHARACTERISTICS, where it reported that the accuracy
of this test was 99.4 percent for fetal sex, the sensitivity and specificity estimates for detecting trisomy 21, 18, and 13 (all in the
90s, some over 99 percent), and "Sex Chromosome Aneuploi-
dies##" (96.2 percent estimated sensitivity; 99.7 percent estimated specificity).

I trusted the people who understood such charts to tell me
what I needed to know. Above the chart, A had written: "Your
NIPT was normal. Please see results and gender below. Congratulations!"

Gabe walked in a few minutes later, and we held each other
in the kitchen and wept. "She's a girl," we'd say over and over and
over again, that day, that week, for months. "We're having a
baby girl."

About an hour later, we drove twenty minutes to a friend's
house in Hillsborough for dinner. On the way, we started hap-
pily brainstorming names. Catherine was Gabe's grandmother's
name, his mom's mom, who'd moved up from North Carolina
to Harlem and raised her family there. Debbie moved to Chicago, where Gabe and his siblings were raised, when she married
Tom, an electrophysiologist who did his residency at the same
hospital in New York where she was a nurse in the '70s. They
have lived in the same brick house on the South Side since before Gabe was born. I'd seen a picture of Catherine in that house,
sitting next to Debbie on the floor in front of a Christmas tree,
and Debbie is pregnant with Natalie. The two women are radiant and nearly identical.

Another name I threw out on that drive was Simone. On

our trip to Chicago that June, the first time I'd met Gabe's mom and his brother, Mike, I'd spent hours rifling through a massive plastic box filled with family photos in their living room. Debbie kept albums and envelopes and Ziploc bags organized with permanent-marker labels like "Gabriel Akiba-Schechter" (his preschool), "Natalie Williams" (pictures of Gabe and Mike at their older sister's college graduation), "Mike soccer" and "Gabriel friends" and "Gabriel soccer" and "Trip to Disney World, 1995." I sat on the living room sofa circled by Tom's four tiny, geriatric dogs looking through every single one, piecing together a history of Gabe's early life.

Also in the box were the kids' high school yearbooks. In Natalie's, her senior page read her full name: Natalie Simone Bump. I said aloud, "I love the name Simone." Gabe was watching a music video his brother had directed on his laptop. They barely looked up.

I remembered that name on that drive to Hillsborough, remembered how it reminded me of Nina Simone, of Simone de Beauvoir, Simone Weil, how elegant it was, how I hoped she'd grow up to be like Natalie: brilliant and cool and idealistic and nurturing. I asked Gabe if it was a family name and he said he didn't know. He said he liked it. He suggested Francine, which is Debbie's middle name, or Poh Poh's name, Lena. I said no to Lena because that was a name a Catholic nun gave to my grandmother when she started attending a missionary school, instead of her Chinese one, which the white teachers couldn't pronounce. My grandmother's maiden name was Liu, and the name was going to be phased out with future generations, as the youngest Lius were women who'd taken their husbands' surnames. "Simone

Liu Bump," I said, and then he said it. We liked it, but we didn't decide anything then; we had so much time.

We got to dinner, ate pizza and salad, told our friends the baby was a girl. Everyone hugged us. One friend said I had to let Q kiss her; I couldn't shield her from germs.

And yet, after that night, we started referring to her as Simone: "When Simone comes," or, when the dogs bounded for me at full speed, "Watch out for Simone." We didn't mean to; it just happened. Within a couple weeks, it had stuck. It was like she'd selected the name herself.

In January, doctors would tell me that the fluid must have begun to build up in her organs by that night.

Over a few weeks that fall, while I lay in bed willing myself not to puke, I shopped online for wedding dresses. I ordered a few in various shapes and fabrics, hated most of them, kept one that looked like an expensive toga, long and drapey, hiding my entire body except for my right shoulder. I held on to that one as an option in case I didn't find anything else.

Around that time, Mom called with an idea: She had a gold qipao that my great-grandmother had had custom-made for herself in Singapore in the '60s; it wasn't a wedding dress, but a family heirloom, a gold, embroidered, knee-length shift dress. She didn't have a picture of it, but she'd bring it the next time she came to visit.

That ended up being in late October, when I was eight weeks pregnant and could barely stay awake for more than a couple of hours at a time and when I was nauseated by the thought of anything except burnt toast and, weirdly, scrambled eggs. When I tried on the qipao, it fit me perfectly. It wasn't meant to be skintight, but the shape of the dress was designed to follow a body closely, a series of delicate buttons cinching closely at the shoulders and up the neck.

I never met my great-grandmother, have only heard my Poh Poh's stories of how her mother would stay out all night playing mah-jongg, and sleep late into the day. How her mother was impossibly elegant, and refined, and materialistic. My mom spent one year living with her in Singapore; she'd called her Wai Poh. We both took in the fact that my body just happened to follow the outline of my ancestor's, three generations later. Of course, my body would soon be changing, and quickly; maybe the qipao wouldn't fit by December. I bought the most extravagant pair of shoes I could find: four-inch stiletto pumps, pink, iridescent and bejeweled, unsuitable for a bride, unsafe for a pregnant one. I loved them beyond reason. I kept the white toga thing, just in case.

Three days after we opened the NIPT results and less than two weeks before our wedding, Gabe and I drove to a large mall to buy him a suit, tie, and shoes for the ceremony. I clutched a box of Carrs as we sized our ring fingers for gold bands, checking Slack on my phone since it was the middle of the afternoon on a Tuesday.

When we got home, I spent a while doing my hair and makeup, and then recorded a short segment to run as part of the *Book Review*'s 10 Best Books of 2022 event. No one at work knew I was pregnant yet, and I couldn't wait to tell them about my daughter.

That night I fell asleep watching *Game of Thrones*, which Tom had persuaded me to watch for the first time that fall, as a distraction from morning sickness. I started from the beginning and made it a little bit past the Red Wedding by the time Simone died, and I haven't been able to turn it on since.

It was the Wednesday before the wedding and I'd just arrived in New York, was eating salad with Mom at her kitchen table. "I couldn't help myself," she said, and went to get a bag from another room. In it were a pink stuffed bunny rabbit, a smaller stuffed bunny attached to a pacifier—in the Chinese zodiac, Simone would be born in the year of the rabbit—and a onesie that seemed far too small for a living human. "This is for six months," she said. "When she's first born, she will be so much smaller than this."

Her phone rang. It was Poh Poh; Gong Gong had fallen in their room at the assisted living facility. "How did this happen?" she asked into the phone, her voice high, like she was out of breath. Poh Poh had been with her physical therapist, in the hallway right outside the room where he was sitting on the couch, where he had apparently tried to stand up on his own, either forgetting or intentionally ignoring his instructions never to do so without calling an aide. As he fell, he'd hit the back of his head against the sharp corner of a side table, hard. He was bleeding heavily; the ambulance was on its way. Only one visitor was allowed, and Mom was his next of kin. She told me to stay home.

One of Gong Gong's last lucid moments involved his sharing a sandwich with Mom in the ER. Turkey or egg salad, she'd asked him, and he'd said egg, held the sandwich himself and ate it, sitting up in a chair. Part of it fell on the floor, and he bent down to get it before Mom told him not to. He pointed to where it was, and she picked it up for him.

He went home to the assisted living facility that night, Wednesday night, and said goodnight to my grandmother as usual. On Thursday morning, when I'd gone out for a walk, Poh Poh called Mom. "He's taken a turn for the worse," Mom told me when I got back. "Poh Poh thinks he had a stroke." When my grandmother had woken up, she saw he too was awake, but he wasn't responding to her at all. They rushed him to the ER once again, Mount Sinai, and this time he would stay the night. No one knew if he was going to make it. I suggested we postpone the wedding. I only wanted to be next to him. Mom didn't want me to go to the hospital for COVID reasons. We pushed off any decisions until we knew more.

Gabe and I had booked a hotel room for ourselves down in Tribeca for that weekend. On Friday I checked in and took the elevator down to the Japanese spa in the basement where I'd also booked a "Little Bean Massage" for pregnant clients. The therapist had me lie face-down on a bolster with a large hole in the center, where the belly would have gone, if I'd had one yet.

"Congratulations," she said, in the identical choreography of so many conversations I would have over the next two months. "Your first?" "How far along?" "Do you know if it's a boy or a girl?"

I went upstairs and showered in the antique-looking bathroom. I ordered myself room service lunch. Before it arrived, Emily knocked on my door. She had not only flown halfway across the world to celebrate with us, she had also booked a room in this same hotel. We sat opposite each other on velvet armchairs and shared roast chicken and salad and crispy potatoes and talked about her new boyfriend, whom she'd met on her favorite holiday, Halloween, she the bride of Frankenstein and he an avocado. We talked about the friends they had in Abu Dhabi and the book she was working on, a mystery novel about a murderous housewife in Cold War Rome. We talked about my pregnancy, how bad the nausea had been, how much better I was feeling just in the last week, how excited and also nervous I was to see so many people at once. How afraid I was that my grandfather was going to die.

We took a cab to a Oaxacan restaurant on Lafayette Street, where my closest friends and cousins sat around a long narrow table and ate short rib tacos and tlayudas and mole and took pictures with a pink Polaroid camera Liz or Caroline brought. We drank virgin and regular margaritas, and halfway through the meal Caroline said they had a surprise for me, and that I was "probably going to think it was stupid."

She pulled out a flat tin box, and it was empty. She told me to pass it around the table, and as I did, each person put something into it.

Caroline put in two sheets of stickers—a stork, a pink onesie, a rattle, and a bottle, one that had HELLO BABY! printed on it in script. She put in flavored lip balms and a picture of me and Liz and her when we were five and three and two, all wearing matching long-sleeved green velvet dresses Poh Poh made for us for Christmas. Liz and I are holding hands and we have bows in our hair. Caroline is too young to hold a pose like we can; she instead crouches down in the left part of the frame, her hand in her mouth. In another picture we are older, on my bed in the Sixty-Fifth Street apartment; I'm on my stomach with my head in one hand and Caroline is lying directly on top of me, temporary tattoos gilding both of her round cheeks. Liz sits upright behind us, stoic and mature.

Liz went next. She put in a pack of Phase 10 cards, the game our family played so many nights we spent together, around dining tables and on carpets and on hot stones next to hotel pools; and professional portraits her photographer had taken of the three of us at her own wedding, in Malibu that February. A black-and-white photo of the three of us at Caroline's college graduation in 2014. A photo of all four grandchildren feeding the ducks around the community pond at Wellesley Town Hall one fall. Jamie is six and his blue striped beanie has Scooby-Doo's face on it. Liz and Caroline are both wearing jackets handed down from me.

Lovia put in a printed photo of us from the time we recorded a podcast at the IPIC movie theater at the South Street Seaport. We are standing in front of a black screen that says THE NEW YORK TIMES / THE BOOK REVIEW LIVE all over it, arms and fingers splayed out like we're old-timey Broadway stars, staring hard at each other.

Devin printed a photo from 2014, when I was driving us and our friend Veena and two others from someplace to another in Montauk. A photo of us and Emily laughing at our friend's wedding that August, because a guy kept farting so bad Emily said "the problem might be medical." A photo of me and Devin at some shitty deli in LA, the time she came to visit me shortly after I'd first met Gabe. "You were so happy," she said. "Gabe made you so happy."

Emily was next. She pulled out a sixteen-inch MacBook Pro. "I think I misunderstood the assignment," she said. She angled the large computer to show the table pictures of us riding camels on the beach the time I visited her in Abu Dhabi, us drinking Peronis at an outdoor café in Rome when I was in grad school.

Veena put in pictures of us post-gaming a wedding at a frog-themed bed-and-breakfast in Pennsylvania in August 2017, at three a.m., draped in towels and sheets we'd found in a supply closet somewhere.

My first friend from college, another Kate, had screenshotted our first Facebook messages from the summer of 2007, before we started our freshman year. Our parents had some distant connection and we were anxious to go in knowing people. She read my horrifyingly cringe messages aloud ("Do you know what you want to major in yet?") and the table lost it, not with me but at me. My face was beet red and it hurt from laughing. The conversation went into the box.

North Carolina Kate put in a photo of the first time I met her daughter, then less than two weeks old, on their porch in Durham. As soon as I'd held Georgia, I think the youngest baby I'd ever met, she immediately turned her face toward my right boob and opened her mouth, wetting my cotton dress. Kate put in another photo from just that September, of Gabe and me and Georgia, by then over a year old, on a speedboat her husband had rented to go tubing on Falls Lake in Durham. My left arm is around Georgia, holding her tight as the boat flew across the water, and my right hand is shielding her pale face from the sun. I didn't know it, but I had to have been pregnant.

Adam, my best friend and roommate from grad school, put in a photo of me holding baby Q when she was the size of one hand, and me next to the Christmas tree we were tricked into overpaying for the year we lived together in New York. A photo of us with my mom and brother wearing glow sticks on the Fourth of July, the summer we spent so much time together a family friend told my mom she thought Adam was "the one" for me, not knowing he didn't date women.

Janie, sitting to my right, put in our kindergarten class photo from 1995, all of us wearing identical green plaid jumpers. She looked, in the picture, exactly like her three-year-old son. We'd gone to school together from 1994 until we'd graduated college in 2011.

By the time it got back to me, the box was overflowing with tangible reminders of my life and of the people who gave it meaning. I told Caroline it wasn't stupid.

This day had already involved more social interaction than I'd had in the previous three months combined, but I rallied. When we got to the biergarten in Greenpoint, Gabe was standing at the bar with Jamie, who was holding the largest mug of German ale I'd ever seen, and telling me nonsense about Gabe's friends, to show me that he knew them now. Caroline forgot her ID, and

Sam persuaded the bouncer to let her in anyway. One of Gabe's friends made a big show of wearing a pearl necklace, which he said was a thing now. What felt like fifty-something of our closest friends and family were meeting one another and being happy, and I drank glass after glass of club soda and tried my hardest to stay awake. Gabe and I left way before the night was over, and were asleep by one.

Still in bed on Saturday morning, I got a call from Poh Poh. Gong Gong was stable, his vitals were all strong, they had so far found nothing wrong with him, physically. But he was still unresponsive, and awaiting a CT scan, or maybe the results from the CT scan; in any case he would not be out of the hospital in time for the wedding.

"I don't want you to cancel," she said. "There is nothing any of us can do anyway. This is a happy occasion. I want you to be happy."

I asked if she would be able to come to the wedding. She said, "I wouldn't miss it for the world."

"We're not going to tell him the ceremony happened," she said. "He was really looking forward to it." She'd cut his hair days before he fell; Mom had sent me a photo of him trying on an old black suit, smiling. I'd asked if he understood what he was trying it on for, and both Mom and Poh Poh confirmed. "He said, 'The professor,'" Poh Poh told me. He could barely remember any of his grandchildren's names, but he remembered Gabe teaches in North Carolina.

"Don't cry on your wedding day," Poh Poh said on the phone, when we both already were. "I can be sad and happy at the same time," I said.

I went uptown to get ready in Mom's bedroom with her, Liz, Caroline, and Natalie. Sebastian bought us all fresh bagels and cream cheese and we ate them on the floor of the TV room. Poh Poh gathered us together in her overly formal way; she had something to give each of us. In her hands were three small jewelry boxes, all pieces that had belonged to her mother, she said. Caroline, the youngest granddaughter, got a jade pin in the shape of a monkey, the zodiac sign they both shared. Liz and I got similar-looking rings, hers a ruby, mine a sapphire ("Something blue," Poh Poh said). We all hugged and thanked her, ogling our gifts and asking about her mother, when she wore these, to what occasions. Caroline started to cry. I got cream cheese on my makeup. We were all so happy.

When I tried on the qipao, suddenly I hated how it looked on me. There was the beginning of a bump, but I didn't look so much pregnant as just puffy. Two hours before I got married I decided what I would wear: the clean and simple one-shoulder gown that left no evidence that I even had a body. I changed in my mother's closet as I had so many times before, before school or a party, borrowing her expensive and meticulously organized clothes or shoes without asking. This backup dress felt like a fancy nightgown, and I was comfortable.

I heard voices start to accumulate downstairs, the caterers passing around champagne and sparkling water. I heard my brother's voice, Gabe's parents' voices, then Gabe's. Upstairs we were taking pictures on our iPhones, my grandmother in her brilliant blue qipao, surrounded by her daughter and granddaughters, fixing nonexistent flaws in one another's makeup and hair.

When the cello and violin were beginning to play downstairs, I noticed my sapphire ring was no longer on my left pinky finger. The ring had been too small for my right ring finger, and I couldn't wear it on my left, where my wedding ring was about to go. It had been loose on my pinky, and now it was gone, and I was on my hands and knees, white gown on the ground, searching everywhere in the apartment I'd possibly been.

My cousins got involved, and when my uncle found us, he did too. He promised not to tell his mother. "It's here, you haven't left the house. It's here." Natalie later said she couldn't forget the image of Uncle Mark in his expensive black suit, combing through the trash bins in the upstairs bathrooms. "Sapphire-gate," she calls it.

I was afraid to tell my mom. I lose everything, from a Carmex to my phone to my house keys to, one time, my car. This was the exact reason I had told Gabe not to buy me an engagement ring; I could not handle the pressure of holding on to something so valuable. (I know exactly where the yellow diamond necklace is right now.)

Mom summoned me to the top of the stairs, where she would walk me down to my husband. I told her, tears starting to form, that I'd lost the ring Poh Poh had given me less than an hour earlier. She wasn't angry. "It's here, we will find it," she said. "Now please just go get married."

I teetered down the stairs in my four-inch heels, and at the bottom, standing in the foyer in tears, was my father. He'd driven across the country to be there, and he looked weary, but there was a big smile on his face. Baldwin held his father's hand as he violently hurled his basket of flower petals onto the living room floor, to the whole room's great amusement.

Beneath an archway of white flowers, before our two families all seated in one room together, Gabe and I wrapped Simone in the folds of our vows, promising ourselves to this family we were building. After taking pictures, we sat around one square table in the dining room, tiny candles hanging from branches of the floral centerpieces, eating and talking and laughing together. My mother gave a toast to welcome everyone to her home and to welcome Gabe, her second son, into her family. My father stood up and told the room, with great eloquence and vulnerability, that I'd taught him more about parenthood than any child should ever have to teach her father. It was a beautiful thing to say, and I also felt it to be true. I thought of the year I'd spent in Los Angeles, sharing our various pizzas, getting to know each other as adults the way we never had when I was a child. I thought of the afternoon I'd been so anxious I called him, and he drove three hours up from Carlsbad to sleep on my couch. After we said good night and Q and I had gotten into bed, there was an earthquake. Not a bad one, it just felt like a very large truck had hit a pothole right in front of the house, but Q hid under the bed, and my dad came in to check if I was okay. If he hadn't been there, there's no chance I would have fallen asleep.

Uncle Mark lightened the tone by sharing a story about the time he lived in Chicago in his twenties and naively chose to park his car on the roof of a parking garage, not understanding why it would be free. He'd spent hours trying to peel the ice from his windshield, trying to dig the car out from the feet of snow so he could drive it. Mom was friends with a fancy caterer who made us tiny grilled cheese sandwiches with truffle oil, appetizers of warm vegetables with some kind of "dust" on the plate, miso cod and short ribs, and a dessert that was some kind of green apple semifreddo, but in the shape of a candy apple on a stick. Simone was not just there in that room; she made every bit of this night happen.

Afterward everyone except my grandmother and Baldwin piled into several cabs and arrived at a cramped bar in the West Village where our best friends had gathered to drunkenly toast us, where our sisters and cousins gave heartfelt toasts and our brothers gave drunken, embarrassing ones, where we ate chocolate cake with vanilla frosting and I immediately took off my insane shoes.

When everyone left to go wherever else they were headed for the night, Gabe and I went back to our hotel. It was December and I hadn't brought a coat, so I put a sweatshirt that said CHICAGO on it over my wedding dress. Before changing into pajamas, Gabe took a picture of us holding up our left hands, showing off our matching gold bands. My makeup is destroyed and I look borderline sick, but I still love to look at it.

Our alarms were set for before five a.m. so we could make a seven o'clock flight to the Dominican Republic. The long, winding drive from the airport to our hotel brought me very close to vomiting, but I didn't. When we got to our room, we passed out for three hours cocooned in the thin veil of the mosquito net hung over the bed, as an extra guard against Zika virus.

Over the next four days Simone and I would read three books, swim in two different pools, and eat, finally eat, things I'd missed after three months of buttered toast and ginger ale: guacamole and snapper and waffles, a giant, juicy pomelo Gabe and I ripped apart with our hands for the three of us to savor together. Gabe drank mamajuana and told every single waiter I was pregnant. It was a small hotel, and we saw the same staff again and again; I listened as they told us about their children, how many they had, how tired they were, how crazy in love, how we'd want two, how we'd want three, how we'd never know love like that until it hit us.

By December 19 we were back in North Carolina and driving to Durham for our first "Centering" class—a program my ob-gyn practice offered in which patients who were due around the same date would come together for group appointments and meetings. The midwife touted its benefits, including community building and the reduction in rates of postpartum depression. I referred to it as group therapy.

We took the elevator up to the second floor of a small office building in a shopping center, checked in with the front office, and took two seats in the waiting area. There were several other couples sitting there too, quietly. One guy was reading Toni Morrison; his wife *Bringing Up Bébé*. I listened as the incoming group members checked in with the receptionist, telling her their names and birthdays as I had.

Soon we were all ushered down a long hallway into a cramped room with chairs arranged against three of the walls, in a U-shape. When all the seats were filled, there were something like eight couples and one woman who said her husband would not be able to come to most sessions because he was a doctor. Besides me and Gabe, everyone, including the two midwives, was white.

A, the midwife who'd handled my nine-week appointment and NIPT, was the leader of these sessions. First she told us to weigh ourselves on the scale outside the room, take our own blood pressures manually (the device never worked; it told every single one of us we had hypertension), and then lie down on a cushioned table in the corner where she would listen for the baby's heartbeat.

I felt mildly self-conscious about stepping on a scale and recording the number in a line full of strangers, and even more self-conscious lifting my shirt and lowering my pants on the table in front of this room of strangers, less the other women than their husbands, who made awkward conversation as their wives swirled around the room measuring themselves.

I'd bought the reasoning that this class would make expectant mothers feel less alone, and I had mostly decided to join it because I thought I might make friends in North Carolina outside of Gabe's academic circle, which hadn't been easy for me working from home every day. But months later, Gabe explained it as a way for the practice to treat more people at once, and this made so much more sense. These appointments would replace a great number of individual visits, since we were taking and recording our own vitals, all in the space of an hour or so. In every single Centering class I attended, my daughter was getting sicker and sicker, and there was no way of detecting it in that room.

On the table, A measured what the midwife called my "fundal height," the distance from my pubic bone to the top of my uterus. As the pregnancy progressed I would learn to measure this myself too, she said. I then waited for A to find Simone's heartbeat, the doppler loud enough for the small room to hear every baby's particular rhythm. "It always takes a second," A said, but could you imagine if she couldn't, one day, for one mother, what she would do or say to that woman, in front of all those strangers?

When we'd finished all the rounds, we sat back down and went around in a circle saying our names, our due dates, what number pregnancy this was for us, if we knew the sex, and a fun fact about ourselves.

"I'll go first," she said from behind her mask, her Carolina accent thick and maternal. "I'm A, I'm not pregnant and don't plan to be ever again; my little ones are five and three. I don't catch babies anymore either; I wanted to spend more of my time doing this kind of prenatal care with y'all instead."

Gabe was the first person to her left. He introduced himself as my husband and said this would be his first child and that we were having a girl. I don't remember his fun fact.

I said my name, that my due date was June 9, and that I'd just moved from New York.

It turned out that everyone in the class was pregnant for the first time except for the woman to my left, who was on her third. She seemed both very proud of this fact and very tired, and she made it clear how difficult the whole process was in ways the rest of us could not know firsthand. A few couples were waiting until birth to find out the sex.

When it got back to A, she laid some ground rules: Everything we said in this room stayed in this room, and it was important to maintain a judgment-free space for all of us. Since we were all due between mid-May and mid-June, she said, we were all past the twelve-week mark, which meant our chances of miscarrying were now dramatically lower than they had been in the first trimester. That didn't mean they were zero. It was possible, she warned, that someone in this room would stop coming. If this happened, A would reach out to that couple and ask for their permission to tell the rest of the group what had happened. The tone of the room became, very briefly, grave and terrifying. You could feel the room collectively try to shake it off, this reminder of lurking tragedy, as A moved on to handing out our spiral-bound workbooks.

In these we were to keep a log of our weights, blood pressures, etc., to chart our progression over the course of the pregnancy. One section explained portion sizes of common foods, and I went ahead and skipped right over it. Another explained pretty crucial information about sexual and dental health and drug use during pregnancy. We would be tested for STDs and STIs; and we should not skip a dental exam because there was now a higher concentration of blood vessels in our gums, and any kind of oral infection could lead to adverse health effects for the baby. Also, we were told, there was no actual proof that marijuana use had any effect on fetal health—because it is unethical to test such things on pregnant people—but if any was found in a baby's bloodstream at birth, the baby could be taken away by child services.

"I'm telling you these things because I have to," A said, almost defensively I felt, justifying giving us knowledge that I was genuinely glad to have. She explained that this curriculum had originally been designed for lower-income families, of which there did not seem to be any present. I wanted to ask why only lower-income people would need to know about gonorrhea and weed, but I didn't.

Finally, the section on exercise. "It is an old wives' tale that women need to be on bed rest throughout pregnancy," A said. "You should feel free to be as active as you feel capable. Who here has been exercising? Show of hands."

Not many hands. The consensus was that over the past nine weeks, we'd felt lucky to be able to walk to the fridge. A said she understood. The woman whose husband was a doctor raised her hand and said she'd been lifting. She and A seemed to share a bond over this.

A told the rest of us to try to move at least a little bit every day. She suggested a walk at night, even just around the block or up and down the stairs at home. Something about our metabolisms after dinner and before bed, I don't remember. I noticed one woman start furiously jotting this note to herself in her workbook.

After the meeting, a few of us stayed back to give another blood sample that would be tested for spina bifida. It was explained to us matter-of-factly that the legal limit for termination in the state was twenty weeks, so some of us might want to gather genetic information on our children before then. I ignored the twenty-week thing; I just wanted as much information as possible about who and how Simone was.

I'd stayed uncharacteristically quiet throughout this first meeting, uncomfortable and vaguely irritated. Afterward, the woman who lifts told us that her Reddit thread said NIPT tests could be inaccurate. I wanted noise-canceling headphones.

I had gone into this first meeting hopeful, thinking I loved group therapy. But this was nothing like the eating disorder treatment I'd done two years earlier. Three days a week I'd sign into Zoom to see roughly the same fifteen faces—some were at the tail end of their sessions when I started, some began as I was ending—all women, from age fourteen to their midfifties, representing a variety of body types and stages of recovery, there because they were desperate or miserable or because their parents were forcing them to be.

At some point in the four-hour sessions it would be mealtime. The program had adjusted its outpatient procedures during CO-VID, so we all prepared our full, balanced meals per that day's instructions off-camera, and then ate together on camera while we tried to simulate "normal" dinner-table conversation about anything other than food or bodies. At the end of these meals, the facilitators would check our plates one by one; I suppose someone could have cheated, but it would have been hard, and I didn't want to. Some women wouldn't be able to finish their meals, and they'd say so at the end, and we'd talk about it. We all had our own disorders, our own myths we wove about food and its relationship to our bodies; but the abject honesty in that "room" was a salve. It felt better to be scared together than alone. We empathized with one another's pain, supporting ourselves, collectively, through it. We weren't allowed to exchange last names or contact information, but I still consider my relationships with those women on my computer screen some of the most intimate I've ever built.

This was not how I felt about Centering. Yes, there was significant anxiety in the group, but it was treated as a side effect as opposed to a focus. The overwhelming mood of the sessions was one of excitement—mine included—but also more than a little pride. It was like we'd all accomplished something, sitting in that sanitized room with our husbands and our fundals and our fun facts, when all we'd done, actually, was have sex and be lucky. If our pregnancies were going well, it wasn't because of anything we'd done, I guess besides not doing cocaine? I was uncomfortable in the feeling that I was taking part in some kind of ritualistic back-patting—even when I was still lucky too.

I flew back to New York a few days before Christmas to spend time with Gong Gong, who hadn't recovered any of his cognitive functioning since the fall before the wedding. I went straight from LaGuardia to the assisted living facility and sat in the room with my mom and grandmother as they tended to my grandfather, unresponsive in the hospital bed that'd been set up in the same sitting room where he'd fallen weeks before.

He was so thin, and he did not speak; his mouth was dry from hanging open for three weeks. He had a catheter he kept trying to pull out, and his strength was surprising when we fought to stop him. My grandmother asked how I was feeling, urged me to go home to sleep, referred to my pregnancy as my "condition." You need sleep, in your condition. You shouldn't be flying, or exercising, or weeping, in your condition. That night and for many thereafter, four generations of women sat at this man's bedside worrying and wondering about the end of life, and the beginning.

On Christmas Eve, Jamie and I went to Whole Foods to buy

groceries for the next night's dinner, and then to see our grand-parents. My grandmother ate dinner at five p.m. in the restau-rant on the first floor of the facility, and she needed someone to watch over Gong Gong during that time. The aides, she com-plained, did not check on him often enough; by the time they noticed he'd pulled his catheter out or fallen off the bed from squirming, it would be too late. My brother and I relieved her so she could eat her steamed salmon and sweet potato downstairs.

There was one chair by his bed, and my brother sat in that while I wheeled back and forth in a wheelchair by the large win-dow. Jamie turned on the TV, I think to drown out the silence, and he found *Men in Black II*. Gong Gong was not squirming tonight, was not exhibiting any discomfort or frustration. He just lay there, eyes closed or slightly open, looking at each of us and usually straight ahead, at the ceiling. A doctor had put him on painkillers and Lorazepam, and I wasn't sure why, other than to make him easier to manage. His head wound had pretty much healed, and anyway was never causing him enough pain to war-rant oxycodone; ditto the catheter. At one point that night, Gong Gong opened his eyes and raised his left arm in a kind of goal-post position, his hand in a fist, a revolutionary demonstrating his allegiance to the cause.

On Christmas Day, Mom had Jamie and me gather in the liv-ing room to exchange gifts and open our stockings. Yes, I am thirty-three and my brother is twenty-five and my mother still endeavors to make every single Christmas as special for us as she did when we were eleven and three. We acknowledged out loud this stocking would be my last; in my mother's house, you get to be a child until you have one.

Jamie got a red electric stand mixer and flannel shirts. I got beautifully framed photos from our wedding and a stocking with SIMONE embroidered on it. We both got a bag of chocolate-covered pretzels and gingerbread cookies. I gave my mom a gold necklace that said WAIPOH on it, the name Simone would call her. "Next year we'll have Christmas with a six-month-old," we said. We didn't say "We may not have Gong Gong."

At ten a.m. we went back to see my grandparents. When we arrived in their room, Gong Gong was no longer in bed, but in a wheelchair, sitting up though staring ahead kind of blankly. My grandmother's favorite aide was dressing him in a bright red sweater and darker red corduroy pants, and we wheeled him down to the first-floor restaurant for the holiday brunch buffet.

At the table, watching Mom and Poh Poh spoon-feed my grandfather things he didn't have to chew—a pot of yogurt, a runny egg—I said to my brother that I wished Gong Gong could enjoy Christmas; he'd always loved Christmas. Jamie put a fist in the air like our grandfather had last night, when he was high as a kite. He said, "I think Gong Gong's having the best Christmas of any of us."

The next night, Mom and Jamie and I took an Uber to Forest Hills, in Queens, to have dinner with Natalie, her husband Chris, and Baldwin. Throughout the dinner Natalie implored Baldwin to "be gentle with Auntie Lauren," because he "didn't want to hurt Simone."

He'd make his hand flat like a pancake and sort of wipe my belly, full of Dan Dan noodles and chicken dumplings and purple yam buns.

"Simone's in there?" Baldwin asked, pointing at my belly button.

"Yes," I said.

"Why?" he asked.

"Because it's safe in there," I tried. "She has to stay in there until she's ready to be born, like you came from your mommy's tummy when you were a baby."

He pretended to be a baby in Natalie's lap and then moved on to playing with the hood of my winter coat, which was lined with a fake fur he was really into pulling.

Natalie said, "Win, can you tell Auntie Lauren what we play in the bath sometimes?"

"Simone," he said, his mouth making a perfect O and then breaking into an embarrassed little smile. Natalie said he'd started pretending, at bath time, to teach Simone about water, about his fish-shaped bath toys, about getting clean.

At one point he grabbed me around the neck and planted a wet kiss on my cheekbone. "I love you," he said. I told him I loved him too.

Before we left the restaurant we exchanged a couple of presents: the set of Legos we'd bought Baldwin, designated for ages four and up (when Chris told him it said that, Baldwin replied loudly, "But I can do it when I'm three") and the hoodie Chris had bought for Gabe, a limited-edition collaboration between Dapper Dan and the Gap that said "DAP" in large letters on the front. He'd gotten one for Natalie and Mike too, in red plaid and black-and-white houndstooth. The one Chris handed to me now for Gabe was dark green plaid, like the fabric of my grade-school uniform.

It was so big and comfy I wore it the next morning on the flight to Utah, and I've basically never given Gabe a chance to wear it since. That week, while my mom and brother skied through a blizzard that piled a hundred inches onto the ground, Gabe and I spent the week in the lodge, working and reading and writing and watching scary movies and eating penguin-shaped chocolates someone sent my mom. Some days we went to the gym together, where he would run while I walked slowly, listening to an audiobook. "Lauren, you're showing," he said to me for the first time on that trip, when I took my jacket off after we got back from the gym one of those days. He looked at my body with a kind of wonder I'd never seen before, and I felt proud.

I decided to try to ski one day, the first sunny day with high visibility, confident enough in my ability to feel safe. We took easy groomed runs and Jamie and our family friend Steve flanked me so that nobody else could knock into me. Gabe had skied for the first time with us the winter before, and he had improved a lot since, but he was still learning. I imagined Simone inside me begging me to go faster, to which I responded, "We have to slow down for your dad!"

On our first night in Utah, in bed with the lights off, I told Gabe how happy I was. "I want to stop time, right now, when everything is just beginning," I said, "when we have everything to look forward to. At some point in our lives, we will not be this happy." I envisioned tragedies like our parents eventually dying, or one of us getting sick, years down the line. Who would we be then? I wanted to name this moment in the present, when I felt we were at the beginning of our life together, Gabe, Simone, and me, but it had barely even started. Our infinite possibilities hadn't yet narrowed into a single, unchangeable past.

My family dog, Archie, had been diagnosed with stomach cancer that September, and his appetite had been slowly fading since. Jamie had brought "the boy" home from Pets on Lex when he was in high school, and now that he'd moved out he went up to Mom's apartment often to spend time with him that fall. To get him to eat, they'd had to up the ante: frozen chicken nuggets, hamburgers from Shake Shack, deli sandwiches from Pastrami Queen. A lifelong food stealer, Archie would stare agog at this food being handed to him and start trying to wolf it down before realizing his stomach didn't actually want it after all. He became so thin you could see the ribs beneath his shaggy blond coat.

While we were in Utah, Archie died. Jamie and Mom came in from skiing and I saw my brother cry for the first time in my adult life, standing in the stuffy locker room with the snow dripping from all our helmets.

We flew home two days later—Mom and Jamie to New York, Gabe and I to North Carolina. When we left each other at the Salt Lake City airport, I cried like a small child, missing my mom and brother already. Missing Archie, worrying my Gong Gong would be next.

We hadn't planned it this way, but by the following Saturday I was back in New York. Gong Gong too had stopped eating, and my mom explained that this was how it would end.

Everyone in my family who'd gathered for the wedding just a month earlier came together in New York once again. For the last moments of his long life, Gong Gong had the people he loved most around him: his wife and daughter and son, his four grandchildren and their partners, his one unborn great-granddaughter.

For several days, our family hovered between my mom's kitchen table and the eighth floor of the assisted living facility, where we took turns cramming into Gong Gong's small hospice room while the others lazed around the lounge down the hall, ordering food and watching football and taking off our shoes and yelling over one another about nothing. One day we sat around for hours discussing the Chinese zodiac sign of everyone in the family—comparing ourselves to one another in meaningless and affectionate ways.

Gabe and Liz and Sam were all born in 1991, the year of the goat. Poh Poh and Caroline are both monkeys. I am a snake, which we all agreed sucked. We discussed the relative merits and drawbacks of the various signs, what we hoped our future children would be. Caroline read aloud a dubious website's description for a rabbit, to predict what Simone would be like. There was something about her being "delicate," which I said I disliked and could already sense would not turn out to be true.

Gong Gong was a dragon. Families in China actually planned their pregnancies in an effort to give birth during the year of the dragon, my mom said. It is the luckiest of the twelve, connoting a giftedness, an essential goodness, a natural eminence. Half-joking, I said I wanted a "dragon boy," a son after Simone, who would grow up to be just like our grandfather. "You were the one who said over and over this fall that you were 'never ever doing this again,'" Gabe reminded me, and I agreed it'd be a tight turnaround. Now that the first trimester hell was behind me, I almost enjoyed being pregnant, the sense of optimism and purpose it gave me, that I was building something, someone, realer than anything I could imagine. I pictured Simone being a big sister.

One of the facility's managers would later tell my grand-mother that they'd never seen so many family members gather for a dying resident before. We joked that if Gong Gong could speak, he would probably tell us all to shut the fuck up ("Why is everyone staring at me and screaming?"). Of course, had he been lucid, we knew he'd have just sat there listening, observing every-one from behind his huge wire-framed glasses, laughing when we laughed, interjecting in the moment you least expected it to say the weirdest or the funniest or the smartest thing you'd ever heard.

I held his hands a lot that week; they were wrinkled and deli-cate, his nails overgrown, and I remembered how I used to watch this same right hand draw things for me as a child. He had been an architect for many decades, and a trained calligrapher before that, and his sketches were works of art. On my visits to Welles-ley, where they lived in a house my grandfather designed him-self, I would bring him a piece of paper and a pencil at the glass table in the sunroom and ask him for a dog, or a girl, or a sun. I wanted to copy his drawings to learn to make them myself—though I would only end up frustrated with my complete lack of skill. He would take the pencil and hold it almost horizontally over the page, hover it over one spot and shake it back and forth ever so slightly before allowing it to land, to make a mark. My

Gong Gong was careful, and patient, and never acted before he'd thought through the action beforehand, never spoke before he knew exactly what to say.

"He's a lucky man," Gabe said the night before Gong Gong died. "We should all be so lucky to be surrounded by so much love as we go."

At 7:45 on the morning of Tuesday, January 10, Gabe and I were asleep in my childhood bedroom when my mom knocked on the door and appeared in the doorway wearing her purple long-sleeved pajamas with white piping around the edges, a dark figure backlit by the bright hallway light. All she said was my name, and all I said was "Oh no."

Neither inside nor outside the room, she said a little too loudly, "He's gone," and then rushed off to wake up everyone else. The facility was a half mile from the apartment, and after we were dressed my cousins and our husbands and I made the cold, quiet walk up Second Avenue one final time—the same walk I'd done back and forth so regularly in those last few weeks.

When we got to their room, on the eighth floor at the end of the hall on the right, their door was ajar as always, so the aides could come and go without my grandparents having to hear a doorbell. Mom was already there; she and my uncle had taken a cab ahead of us.

I hugged my grandmother and we both cried. I went into his room and saw his body, his mouth agape like it always was when he fell asleep on the couch. His hands were folded neatly on his belly, and when I held one it was still warm. There were exasperated exchanges between Mom and Poh Poh and my uncle Mark regarding the funeral home and whatever city officials whose job it is to come issue an official death certificate. We surrounded him in that small room once again, in death as we had in life, my family members constantly offering me one of the few chairs in the room, because I was the pregnant one, the one who shouldn't cry, who should be thinking of the baby.

I would tell Simone about this, I thought. How she'd never gotten to meet him, but how she'd been right there with me, beside Gong Gong, at the end of his life. How he'd known about her before he went. How this was the greatest grief I'd yet known, but it was exactly as it should be: an old man dying after a long, full life; and his great-granddaughter on the precipice of hers.

We watched his body get wheeled away into a large freight elevator. We left the facility for the last time. I don't remember the walk home. Somewhere, Gong Gong was cremated. I thought about a friend's mother's funeral three summers ago, when we'd watched as the funeral home staff ushered the mahogany casket into a large oven and shut the doors. She'd had breast cancer; per Hindu tradition, her husband and two daughters had worn all white for the preceding ceremony. At the crematorium, we could see the bright orange fire through a small sliver.

When the urn carrying my grandfather's remains was ready, Mom and Gabe went to a funeral home somewhere on First Avenue to pick it up. It was heavy, and she couldn't carry it alone: It was a large, round, navy marble jar. The Uber had taken longer than they'd expected, Mom told us, and they'd been waiting on the sidewalk for minutes when she looked at Gabe and said, "Please don't drop that."

Mom, Jamie, Gabe, and I took an Uber to Williamsburg to

have dinner with Caroline and Sebastian, Liz, Sam, Mark, and Michelle. On the way over we passed Peter Luger, and Gabe and Jamie wanted to go there while we were in New York. They tried to call and make a reservation. "Tell them we're grieving," Mom said.

"Our grandfather just died," Gabe told the host. "This was his favorite restaurant." We laughed in the backseat; my grandfather had never heard of this Brooklyn steak house, let alone been to it. Still, I envisioned him eating there, loving it as much as he loved anything else in life, taking it in, gratefully, tucking in his napkin between the top two buttons of his shirt.

The host didn't take the bait, and we still haven't been to Luger's since. But every time I pass it I think, Gong Gong's favorite restaurant.

That night, in my bed with the lights off, a superstitious fear entered my brain. "You know how deaths come in threes?" I said to Gabe, who was lying next to me, possibly asleep. "Archie, Gong Gong. What if Simone is next?" I asked it like I've always asked my deepest fears to anyone who will listen: What if I throw up? What if Mom goes to work one day and never comes home? What if my daughter dies before I do? As if I can call out the future before it happens; as if by naming it, I can remove it from the realm of random bad luck. As if I have any power at all to prepare myself for the worst.

A couple of days later, when we were still in New York, Gabe said to me, out of the blue, "Remember what you asked me the other night, about how deaths come in threes?" I told him I did. "Hootie. The third death was Hootie's."

We returned to Chapel Hill on the Sunday after Gong Gong died, since we had our next Centering meeting on Monday. I brought a large water bottle in a canvas tote bag, along with a bag of crackers and a brand-new red leather planner I'd bought myself for the new year. I'd already written "DUE DATE" on Friday, June 9, in capital letters boxed in a rectangle with three stupid hearts next to it.

When I sat down at Centering—everyone took pretty much the same seats, at least the three times we went—I opened the bag to find that the water bottle had drenched the leather notebook. Gabe took the whole bag to the bathroom to wipe everything off.

That meeting involved filling socks with rice—a microwavable heating pad for us to take home and put on our aching limbs and ligaments—and little index cards with symptoms on them laid out on the floor. A instructed us to each pick up two symptoms we'd experienced in pregnancy, and then we went around to share, commiserating with one another on our lower back pain, exhaustion, and discharge. Except I didn't have any discharge, hadn't since very early on in the pregnancy. I noted it but didn't think anything of it.

At some point A asked the room if we'd felt our babies move yet. We were all between eighteen and twenty-four weeks, the window in which you're supposed to start feeling little "flutters," and I hadn't experienced that either. That did make me nervous, but I was just twenty weeks; I'd had a lot going on and it can be hard to notice when they're that small. There was still time. We brought the rice sock home in my damp tote bag with my damp planner.

That Saturday, Gabe and Simone and I went to see UNC play NC State at the Dean Dome. Gabe had bought season tickets in his second year there; but given my symptoms and the new puppy, this was the first time either of us had gone. Our seats were very high up, and I got breathless walking up the narrow steps, dizzy looking down at the tiny teenage celebrities on the court. We cheered as our team led, and when our team won. We did not boo the small children playing for the other team, like our full-adult neighbors in the nosebleeds did. In the second half one of the NC State starters got very hurt on the court, so hurt he had to be medevaced out.

We walked back from the stadium to our house, alongside a horde of drunk students, and I again lost my breath trudging up the hill.

The next day was the AFC Championship, and the Bills were playing the Bengals to go to the Super Bowl. Gabe used to live in Buffalo and Chris grew up there. He and Natalie had sent me a royal blue T-shirt that said LET'S GO BUFFALO on it, and I sent them a picture of myself wearing it. The Bills lost.

That Sunday was also the first night of Chinese New Year—the year of the rabbit, Simone's year—and our friend Daniel's birthday. His wife, Laura, had just had foot surgery, so we offered to bring over dinner, and our other friend Angeline made a birthday butter cake with fresh whipped cream.

I made Poh Poh's recipes for sesame noodles and a cucumber salad that I'd always loved growing up, and Gabe made a slow-cooker short rib with ginger and soy sauce. I made Laura a plate of food and brought it over to her armchair in the living room, her two feet in casts on an ottoman in front of her. We ate on the couches by the fireplace and talked about TV shows and my grandfather's death and our anatomy scan, scheduled for the next day. My belly was now visible, and Gabe liked to point it out to everyone.

The next day, Monday, I was twenty weeks and three days pregnant. I took Q on a walk around the neighborhood and the sun was so strong I had to take off my winter jacket. I felt self-conscious without it in my leggings and tight turtleneck, my body growing more and more distended by the day.

Multiple friends who had babies had told me to look forward to this scan, the twenty-week scan, that it was spectacular: I'd see every organ in detail, even get a three-dimensional image of her face. "I can't wait to see her," I'd been saying to Gabe all morning, all week, eager for this day to come.

Before leaving, Gabe opened a package from Hydrow, the company that made the at-home rowing machine he had upstairs.

"Check it out," he said, and showed me a card that congratulated him on a million meters, and a shirt. He put the card on the fridge with a magnet, and it remained there for months as a reminder of the *before*, of our last moments of blind optimism. I asked if we should bring anything to the appointment, but I'm not sure what I meant. "Like a bottle of wine?" Gabe said. We were stupid and giddy.

On the drive over, I played SZA's "Kill Bill," a song about murdering her ex and his new girlfriend, which I cannot bear to hear now. As we pulled in I asked him, in another jolt of instinctive panic, "What if she's not okay?" Another verbal knock on wood. I know now that I said these things—What if this, what if that—not out of pessimism, but out of its opposite. I was preempting fate, I was taking control. Bad things happened, of course, but how often were they the specific things we specifically predicted out loud?

What Gabe said, in the passenger seat, as I turned into the driveway was "Then we'll get through it."

We sat on the luxurious white armchairs in the waiting room of the ob-gyn practice, decorated with pale pink accents, children's books, and framed, abstract drawings of female silhouettes. I chose this practice over those at Duke and UNC because I'd been sold by this serenity, this palpable sense of ease and even buoyancy that the office and staff radiated, this sense that bad things don't happen here.

I was low-risk, everyone said; I had no history of miscarriage, no significant medical history whatsoever, I did not do drugs or smoke or even really drink. I was thirty-three but enjoyed referring to this as my "teen pregnancy." The practice was run by a group of rotating doctors and midwives, all of whom I saw a handful of times in my sequence of appointments. This was all right with me; it was presented as a good thing to get to know as many of them as possible, because you never knew who would be on call when you went into labor.

The same sonographer from last time called us in, and I went to pee before the exam. I came back and got on the table and held Gabe's hand.

For about ten minutes, we watched on the screen as the wand scanned across my belly, beaming at our baby, who had grown so much in the eleven weeks since we'd seen her last. We were two idiots gushing over her hands, her fingers stretching and contracting, a lugubrious kind of wave. "Is that her spine?" we asked. "Is that her heart?" "Yes," the woman said, "yes."

Still, I wondered what my friends had been talking about: I could make out certain organs and shadows of what looked like a body part, but this scan was not very clear at all. Everything looked mostly black. Maybe there was another machine I had to be hooked up to next, or some high-resolution setting that hadn't been turned on yet. But I'd never had an anatomy scan, hadn't even had a basic ultrasound since the nine-week appointment, when there wasn't much at all to see besides a flicker of a heartbeat, maybe a twitch of movement if you were lucky. I wonder if it was denial that made me think, This must be what it's supposed to look like.

But the sonographer did gently say multiple times that she couldn't see what she was looking for either, that the baby was in a weird position that wasn't allowing her an easy view. After several minutes of scanning around for a view that wasn't almost entirely black, she finally said, "I'll let you take a break, flip over onto your side," and calmly got up to leave the room. "I'll come back in a few minutes and maybe she'll have moved by then."

When she was gone I rolled over to face Gabe and still wasn't worried. Later he'd tell me he already was. I remember saying, "I just want her out of me," which is the kind of thing I said a lot, because the whole business of growing a person inside of me freaked me out. And because I was impatient, and couldn't wait to meet her.

The next few minutes felt like they happened in slow motion. Before the sonographer came back into the room, I heard her voice in the hall, telling someone else, "twenty and a half weeks." That was it, those five words, they were the first crack, the tiny cleaving between my old life and a new, crueler, emptier one.

The sonographer came back in with a doctor I hadn't met yet, a woman in dark blue scrubs, her brown hair in a ponytail.

The wand was on my belly again, and now there were two pairs of eyes on the screen, on my child's body and mine, and the despair in those eyes made me want to scream. The sonographer whispered something about not being able to see all the chambers of the heart, which made me imagine a tiny heart with pieces missing.

This is when I spoke, my voice shaking. "Is everything okay?" I said, pathetically, knowing nothing was.

The doctor in the blue scrubs looked at me then, and I wanted to beg her to look back at the computer, to keep looking for the hope I needed until she found it. But she wasted no more time with the scan, because she didn't need to. She walked around the bed to stand on my left side, where Gabe was still sitting.

"I am so sorry," she said, nodding like she knew I knew, her voice caring but firm. "I'm very concerned. The reason we can't see your baby is because there is significant fluid building up in and around her, it's behind her head and throughout her abdomen, blocking her organs." She said something about my baby's arms and legs not "developing properly." She said, "We need to get you to a specialist as soon as possible."

I don't remember what I said. Gabe asked if she'd live.

The doctor said, "I don't want you to go into the hospital with false hope." She said, "This is not what we were hoping to tell you today." She said, "Can I give you a hug?"

I wanted to go to the hospital immediately, I told the doctor, but it was almost five, and that wasn't likely. She left the room to call Duke, and the sonographer held me and said that she would come home with us if she could, wanted to make sure we'd be okay. I believed her. I wanted her to come home with me, pictured her standing in her scrubs in our kitchen. Then she too left the room, and we were alone.

I got off the bed and onto Gabe's lap, needing him to physically anchor me as I lost all connection to the world as I knew it. "I'm sorry," I wailed into his neck, "I'm so sorry, I'm so sorry." I'd failed Simone, failed him. I called my mom and it went to voicemail. "We'll get her down here tonight," he said, and I understood from another angle the magnitude of what was happening.

The doctor returned and said Duke couldn't see me today, it was too late, we'd have to wait for an appointment tomorrow. We left that office without scheduling a next visit, without a plan for any kind of future. Walking through that pale pink waiting room this time, I felt the shame of being a horror story these smiling women would try to forget, or would go to dinner and tell their husbands and friends about, shuddering at the thought of the statistic I'd become. "Once you've been on the losing side of great odds," Elizabeth McCracken wrote in a memoir of the stillbirth of her son, "you never find statistics comforting again."

As we exited the office we were blinded by the glare of a bright yellow sunset, shining directly onto us from straight ahead. The air was crisp, the late afternoon dramatically, hauntingly beautiful. I stopped Gabe right outside the entrance and made him hug me right there, in the sunshine. It is the cliché of the century to say that the instant I saw this sun I felt it was her beaming down on me. But it is also true, and I wanted us to bask in it for a second.

As I walked to the car, my mom called me back. "Mom," I wailed, and the anxiety in her "What?" betrayed the mother's love I now might never experience for myself. She was supposed to go to Miami for work the next day, and London for a board meeting the week after. I don't remember how I told her, what I told her, I knew so little about what was happening then, only that it was terrible. I hung up and told Gabe that she wasn't sure she could come right away, because this was the impression she'd left me with.

We got home, and I said I wanted to take a shower. "Will you leave the door open?" Gabe asked, and I'm still not sure what he was worried would happen if I didn't.

When I got out, he'd already booked Mom's flight from La-Guardia to Raleigh-Durham for that night. He had to go pick up Hopscotch from Green Beagle, the fancy "lodge" where he went for daycare. He asked if I wanted dinner afterward, and I didn't, but when he ordered burritos from Cosmic Cantina, a tiny Mexican restaurant all the students loved, I surprised myself by wolfing down the entire thing. The resilience of my animal hunger was a strange comfort—I was still pregnant, after all, she was still there with me.

My mom landed around ten and Gabe drove to pick her up. "Want to come with me?" he asked. "I'm worried about you being alone." He thought I might hurt myself. I told him I wouldn't.

Alone in bed, I googled "fluid in fetal abdomen." A Stanford Children's Health page gave me my answer right there in the search results: "Hydrops fetalis is severe swelling (edema) in an unborn baby or a newborn baby." *Hydrops fetalis.* How similar are the words fetal and fatal.

I clicked. I read, "Hydrops develops when too much fluid leaves the baby's bloodstream and goes into the tissues." On another website, the one for a children's hospital in Minnesota, I read, "Hydrops fetalis is not a disease, but a symptom of an underlying health problem with the baby. If untreated, the excess fluid can stress the baby's heart and other vital organs, putting the baby's life at risk."

This page was longer. I read, "Immediate delivery of a baby with hydrops fetalis is sometimes needed." I read "mirror syndrome." I read "preeclampsia." Normally a hypochondriac, I don't remember quite processing these threats to my own life at the time I first learned of them. Maybe because my brain was still playing catch up, maybe because I felt—physically—totally fine, maybe because my life in that moment felt beside the point; the only one I cared about was hers.

I called my brother. Jamie hates talking on the phone, so I almost never call him, and maybe that's why when I did that night he answered. I heard voices in the background, so I knew he wasn't alone. He lived with three roommates in Murray Hill, so this wasn't surprising. What was surprising was that he picked up.

I was crying. I told him Simone wasn't going to make it. He took a really deep breath, and I knew he had no idea what to say. I could hear him trying to process this information that was so foreign to him, so outside of his world, and trying to figure out the words I might need to hear. When Gong Gong was dying, Jamie had been by his side every day, making jokes the way he always does when a situation is hard—showing his love by defusing tension, just by being there. When Gong Gong actually died, Jamie was at the facility once again, but now he wasn't making jokes. He hugged everyone and stared hard at the floor. He did not make a big display. He quietly said, "No, that's okay," when Mom asked if he wanted to see Gong Gong's body before they took it away.

Now, on the phone, Jamie said he couldn't believe what I was telling him, and that it "sucked," and that he was sorry. He sounded sadder than I'd ever heard him sound. I asked him if he would come down to North Carolina, and he said he would. I told him I loved him, and for the first time in twenty-five years he said he loved me too—and in front of whichever friends he was with. We hung up.

At some point that night, Debbie called me. I don't remember everything we said, but I remember that her voice was both heavy and soft, and immediately comforting. I told her I felt like

I'd let everybody down, let Simone down. She told me that I hadn't, and then told me something that broke me, but also gave me a reserve of strength I needed so desperately that night, and have needed every night since.

"I don't know if you know this, but I lost two pregnancies before Natalie was born," she said, and I thought in that moment, How did this woman go on? She then had another miscarriage after Natalie was born, before she'd had Mike and then Gabe, pregnancies that required her to be on bed rest for months. All these lost pregnancies made it past the first trimester, but only one had a name: Steven.

"I wish now that I'd named all three of them," she said. "It's good that Simone had a name. She will always be a part of the family."

How had I not considered that such a thing was possible, that a person could endure so much loss in a lifetime?

Before we said goodbye, Debbie told me that I would be angry and sad for a long time, and that people would try to say things to make me feel better, but they wouldn't, and that was okay. She told me this wasn't my fault, which was something I hadn't considered before that phone call either.

She told me that whatever happened, I would survive.

Before getting in bed, I texted Liz and Caroline. I said I was too depleted to call, but that I loved them. "She's still alive right now and I'm taking care of her until she's not," I wrote. That thought was the only one that made any sense to me that night.

They told me they loved me and Gabe and Simone, and I could feel their pain from afar. For months Caroline had been gathering images of mobiles and wall decals and night-lights to design the nursery, which we thought could be bunny-themed for her birth year, the year of the rabbit. I haven't asked Caroline if she still has those images saved somewhere, that room where Simone lives.

I have spent my life attached to my own mother at the hip, in as literal a sense as I could manage. She has always worked, a lot. I didn't like this, felt scared and angry and sad because of it, and I've spent so much of my life trying to communicate that to her, so many times, in so many ways.

From my earliest childhood well into my twenties, the prospect of her leaving me, even temporarily, of being without her and being unable to reach her, caused me significant and persistent and sometimes debilitating anxiety. The immediate fears ranged from throwing up without her around to take care of me to her dying in a plane or car crash; but these were symptoms of a more general insecurity about her presence in my life, an uneasiness with my own independence. They say it takes most babies seven months to understand themselves as individuals separate from their mothers; it took me thirty years.

My earliest memories are of living in Dallas, where Mom and I moved after she and my dad divorced when I was not yet two. She moved there for a job at a department store that required her to travel internationally all the time. I spent a lot of time with a British babysitter, her husband (who was pretty mean to me), and her son, who was around my age and gave me a pair of tiny hand-me-down cowboy boots that I later wore every day to my Manhattan preschool and still have to this day. In Dallas, I was not yet ready for preschool; when Mom tried sending me at two, I sat in a corner by myself all day, crying.

There is a picture from this time of my mother and me on the front lawn of our house. She is sort of squatting down, balancing in her pantsuit and heels, holding me on one of her legs. I am in turn holding my doll, Elizabeth (named after my cousin), who's wearing a purple plaid dress that is identical to mine, one of the many sets of clothes Poh Poh made for us over the years. Mom is looking down at me and I am kissing the back of Elizabeth's bald plastic head and frowning. I vividly remember my grandmother taking this photo, just before Mom got into a car service to take her to the airport for a business trip. Poh Poh would stay and take care of me until Mom got back.

My grandmother still talks about that period as one of unhappiness and loneliness for me. Where my mother tends to brush over emotion like a stone skipping over a river, never pausing long enough to let her weight sink beneath the surface, my grandmother and I skew toward melodrama, and fatalism. "You missed Cory," she'll say now, my dad having disappeared from my life at such a young age I couldn't have understood an explanation even if one had been given. "Your mom was working so much, and you were alone a lot, in this strange place you didn't recognize. Everyone in San Francisco had looked like you and your mom. In Dallas, the other children you saw were all white, and they bullied you."

She's even told Gabe once that she'd been so worried about me in those days that she'd offered to take me in and raise me herself. Mom rolled her eyes when I repeated this to her, asking if it was true. "She exaggerates everything," Mom said. "Were those days perfect? No. Was I gone too much? Yes. But there was never one second of your life when I ever imagined not being in it."

It was around that time that I met my future stepfather, the man I'd call Dad for the next decade or so, long after he and my mother divorced. His job was in New York, so when they got engaged, when I was three, we moved there, first into a hotel and then into an apartment on the sixth floor of a building four blocks south of my preschool. Since she'd quit her job to leave for New York, there was a brief window when we'd first moved when Mom didn't work. She'd walk me those four blocks there and back every day, buying me a big, salty pretzel from the same street vendor on the way home.

When she did start working again, her schedule was unrelenting, and it would only become more so as I got older. I loved to watch her get ready for work in the mornings or for business dinners at night, sitting on the closed toilet seat as she pumped body lotion from a glass bottle onto my legs in the shapes of smiley faces, or sitting on the carpet of her narrow walk-in closet and observing the ways she moved and dressed and the parts of her body that looked so different from mine, assuming that I would look just like this someday too. I spent so much of my childhood admiring her beauty, witnessing the elaborate rituals by which she accentuated it—by which she prepared to leave me—aching for her to stay.

Before leaving, she'd bend down to kiss me goodbye, but instead of kissing my cheek or letting me kiss hers, she'd give me only the bottom of her chin. This was to avoid ruining her makeup, the perfect bright-red stain of her full lips, the careful balance of foundation and blush on her skin. I would end up with some part of my face knocking against the hard bone of her jawline, taking in an intense waft of the perfume she'd just applied to it. I'd stand there watching her until the elevator doors closed, until she was gone.

At six or seven or eight, I'd become so paranoid about her leaving on business trips—sometimes more than a week long, sometimes back to back, to Brazil or Venezuela or Thailand or China or Germany or Washington, DC—that I'd administer a "test" every time she returned, asking her questions only my "real mom" would know the answers to.

If you're not an impostor, I'd ask, then where is the big freckle on my leg? (My left knee, next to the scar I got when I fell off my bike in Poh Poh's driveway when I was three.) What do I wish she'd named me instead of Lauren? (Abigail, because when I was in kindergarten there was a fourth grader named Abigail I thought was cool.) What do I need every night in order to go to bed? (A glass of milk warmed up in the microwave.) Unpacking her suitcase on the white embroidered bed she shared with my stepfather, she'd distractedly ace the test, but I would remain uneasy for days. By the time I forgot about it, she'd have to leave again.

On Sundays before she had to leave for a trip, she'd take me with her to get manicures and pedicures, telling the Korean technicians that I could get whatever design I wanted, which was usually a flower or a butterfly. I tried to focus on my nails instead of the pit in my stomach, sitting in those too-big massage chairs, their violent rumbling shaking me from below.

I was also the kid who never went on sleepovers or to sleep-away camp, and when my mom and stepfather divorced, I started spending the whole night in my mom's bed, a habit that persisted until high school. I think she let me do this because she felt guilty for leaving me so much; or maybe she missed being close to me too.

I was raised by a pretty constant turnover of babysitters, Xi-ying and Carmelita and Maricel and Cecilia and Lee and Yen, women who were fifty-one or eighteen, Malaysian or Filipina or Chinese, women who loved me and were exasperated by me and complained about me and cooked chicken drumsticks and pasta and baby carrots for me and disciplined me and were manipulated by me into buying fruit roll-ups or a pink inflatable armchair after school.

My stepfather gave me an AOL account for Hanukkah in fourth grade, and in addition to instant messaging, I figured out how to access airline websites. On the nights my mom was flying home or away, my babysitter at that time would have to try everything to get me to go to sleep, but I'd refuse, forcing myself to stay awake at the large desktop computer in the kitchen, reloading and reloading the flight page on our dial-up internet until it said the plane had landed, certain that if I did not do this, my mom's plane would crash and she would die.

My babysitter's own son was back in the Philippines; he was eighteen, an age I found impossibly old, and she told me she hadn't seen him since she left for the U.S. when he was a baby. Lee was about four foot nine, but the son I imagined was toweringly tall and skinny, in a bedroom that looked just like Lee's at our apartment but somewhere in Manila, sitting on her bed all alone.

When I was ten, my mother divorced again, and Jamie's two-year-old life became split in two: There was forever a calendar hanging in the kitchen on which every single day was marked with either Mom's initials or his dad's. When they'd been married, they'd had screaming fights in their bedroom, and I'd gather Jamie up from his crib or his playpen and run him to the other side of the apartment, to the kitchen or to Lee's bedroom, and sit with him, play with him, pretending he was my child and we were fleeing some war-torn country. I hadn't realized how lonely I'd been without a sibling until Jamie came; now I had to spend half my life without him again.

From then on, when Mom traveled or stayed out late or left for work early, I no longer had my stepdad at home to eat dinner or breakfast with, to put me to bed or on the school bus. Poh Poh came a lot, on the Chinatown bus from Boston, but traveling got harder for her as she got older. Other times, I stayed with babysitters, who complained about my neediness, my irrational fears and sleeplessness that kept them awake in the middle of the night. I was "a spoiled brat," I heard one babysitter telling someone on the phone, in her room. True! Mom's job paid her excessively, and I had everything any child could ever need or want.

What I didn't feel I had, feel I could count on having, was the only parent I really knew.

This anxiety metastasized into my adolescence and early adulthood, when I would drive home an hour and a half from college every single night because I was too afraid to sleep in my dorm, and when I stopped eating anything that I thought could make me sick (most things) when I did manage to stay away. When she dropped me off for freshman year, she called me from the drive home, sobbing. I was mad at her then, for making my own sadness harder to bear, but I understand it better now. She was just someone's daughter, missing, needing her own. Her sadness was my problem too, and I'm grateful that in that moment, she gave it to me.

College was a struggle. Less the school part than being away from home. The rush I felt when I'd get in my car to come home far outweighed any social benefits I saw to staying on campus, and anyway I had friends in New York. By senior year, I managed to force myself to stay at school, but the only way I was able to do that was by severely limiting what I ate. If I couldn't be near my mother, the illogic went, I couldn't afford to risk being sick. Instead of a baby blanket or a stuffed animal, I coaxed myself to sleep each night with a uniform "snack" that I would eat at the exact same time in the exact same order, a compulsory token onto which I forced a feeling of safety: grapes, an English muffin, a piece of bread, several different kinds of dry crackers broken into deliberate pieces, a cup of dry Cheerios. The ritual of eating this snack, in my dorm room bed, after finishing a paper or coming home from a night out, signaled to my brain that I was okay; I was protected.

Throughout that time I would cling to my mom in new ways, calling her when she was in important meetings to tell her I was having a panic attack, asking her to keep her phone on all night in case I needed to call her, making other such unreasonable demands on her attention to overcompensate for what I felt was a gaping lack of it. None of these tactics worked, in the sense that they did not bring her closer to me. They only contributed to a maturing resentment and misunderstanding between us. She called me selfish for asking for more care than she was giving me. I countered that, emotionally speaking, that was not much at all.

The real effect of all my restrictions, of course, was to put my body in actual, physical danger. I don't trust many of my memories from this time, which was long. I was delusional, and so I cannot tell you if it's true that there were times when my mother praised my appearance and my "willpower"; but she insists there were more conversations in which she expressed a concern over my diminishing body weight, my persistent shivering in eighty-degree heat, my nervous breakdown in any situation that involved a disruption of my "schedule."

By my twenties, I was at least nominally an adult, living on my own, monitoring my own meals and making my own decisions. My life and my body continued to feel like my mom's responsibility in a way that shamed me; but with an anger coagulating out of so much fear, I resolved to take control of it myself. Mom could encourage me to see the demeaning psychiatrist on Eighty-Fifth Street, but I alone decided whether I wanted to take his pills. I didn't want to "cure" my anxiety, because I didn't actually see it as a problem—it was the viruses and bacteria that were the problem, not my response to them. Would taking Celexa make me start eating out of the garbage? As unpleasant as it was to manage, my eating disorder was also the best tool I had for coping with the persistent fear of being alone.

Until, gradually, it stopped working. Then the SSRI, the outpatient treatment program, the slow rebuilding of my relationship with my body's needs. It just so happened around this time that the pandemic grounded my mother from traveling, and she and my brother and I found ourselves under one roof together as adults the way we'd never been when we were younger. The three of us cooked and wiped packages for one another, knew every detail of one another's days in a way that made us both calm and crazy.

In July 2020, with a return to my Eighth Avenue office nowhere in sight, I moved to LA. I didn't see my mother for five months, and with that distance—chosen by me, not her work schedule—our relationship found its balance; we had the space to miss each other, and we did. I have never stopped making my mother's life difficult, with my feelings and my need to talk about them, my impatience and my refusal to let things go. I'm still scared of throwing up, but I no longer think it would help that much to have my mom around if I do. When we are apart, we still feel each other's emotions as our own. We always come back to each other. Sometimes I still bitch at her like a four-year-old, and she lets me.

When Mom and Gabe got home from the airport that first night after we knew Simone was sick, I was in bed with the lights off, but not asleep. She didn't even take her jacket off before storm-ing into my bedroom, sitting on my bed, and hugging me, hard. "If I could take this pain away from you and absorb it, I would," she said into my hair, soaking it in her tears.

"I should have known it was too good to be true," I said through heaving sobs. I felt like an idiot for having believed a miracle like Simone could ever happen.

My mom pulled away, clutched both of my shoulders and looked me straight in the eye. I'd never in my life needed her the way I did in that moment, and she was there.

"It was true," she said of her only grandchild. "And it was good."

The next morning my eyes were swollen from crying and Gabe's father, Tom, arrived from Chicago. Hopscotch barked at him with the big-boy bark he'd just learned, protecting his house from large men. Tom still keeps a demanding patient schedule, so it was a big deal for him to drop everything and show up at our house on a Tuesday.

The four of us sat in our living room while I cried off and on, saying "I can't believe it" over and over and over. I still had not heard from Duke about an appointment, so I texted my friend Katharine, a neonatology fellow at the Children's Hospital of Philadelphia.

"I have no idea what is going on," I told her. "My obstetrician told me nothing. Only that there was fluid inside her and not to have hope. I don't know when I'm going to get an appointment, or if I'm going to miscarry any second. I don't know if she's still alive."

The last time I'd seen Katharine was at the bar after our wedding; she'd been thirty-seven weeks pregnant with her second child, a boy who was now a month old. I heard him making gurgling baby sounds in the background as she nursed him while talking to me. I'd known Katharine since we were kids; our moms had been college friends and we both grew up in New York, went to the same college our moms did, and lived next door to each other senior year. When I was first pregnant, she gave me a set of the Olivia children's books, the name of her daughter—or Olivia gave it to "Baby Bump," saying she couldn't wait to meet her.

"Did they say the word 'hydrops'?" Katharine asked now, her voice a tightrope act between clinician and friend, caring but also confident, profoundly unruffled.

I told her they had not said that word, but that I'd found it on-line the night before. "I know you can't say anything without seeing my scans, knowing any of my obstetrical history," I said. "But as my friend: Is she going to die?"

"I really don't know," she said, and I believed her. "I really hope not, but I don't know. Hydrops is more of a symptom than a diagnosis. It could be an indicator of so many different things. It makes sense that your OB reacted so strongly; it sounds like what they saw on your scan was pretty uncommon, relative to the population. That office probably sees cases like this once every few years. But offices like mine see this kind of thing every single day. It's all we do. You'll feel a lot better when you talk to specialists."

She offered to connect me with the fetal diagnostics center at CHOP. If they could see me immediately, she said, she'd pick me up at the airport, I could stay at her place. This prospect required just enough logistical planning to let me feel like I was in control. I thanked her from the bottom of my heart, hung up, and went back to waiting.

After lunch I got a call from an unknown number in Durham. A soft voice on the other end introduced herself as K, a genetic counselor at the Fetal Diagnostic Center at Duke. She was so sorry to be speaking with me under these circumstances, she said, a refrain I would hear repeated so, so many times over the next week.

She asked if I was available to come in the next morning; I said I was. She outlined the course of the day: I would do another ultrasound, and she and a doctor would meet with me and Gabe to "talk about your options." This phrase encouraged me in a way that it shouldn't have. If your child is dying, I thought, there are no options.

Another reason for her call, she said, was to ask my permission. I'd done the NIPT, right? I said that I had, and that it had been clear. This was not a chromosomal issue, I said with the confidence of a moron.

"Actually, the scans I've seen are giving me reason to suspect a chromosomal abnormality called Turner syndrome, or monosomy X," she said. "It's when a female embryo has only one X chromosome instead of two. It won't necessarily change the prognosis, but it could be useful for you, going forward, to know the cause."

I asked what Turner syndrome meant. Was this the cause of the fluid?

"Yes and no," she said. "Turner itself is not necessarily fatal. The vast majority of embryos that have it are miscarried within the first trimester, but a very small percentage make it to full term. Baby girls born with one X chromosome have normal brain function. They may have chronic heart complications, or trouble conceiving. They may be shorter than the rest of their family members. But otherwise, they can go on to live full, happy lives. The danger is when this chromosomal abnormality affects the child's organs early on, when they are still forming. This organ failure could be what's causing the fluid to build up. But we don't know yet. This is what we'll try to determine when you come in. For now I just need your permission to find out if your blood showed evidence that she could have Turner."

I asked her when I should come in to do another blood test.

"No," she said, "you've already done this test. I just need permission to look at the results that are already there."

I was too afraid then, back when Simone was still alive, to understand the full weight of what K was telling me. I made my confusion clear.

"The best way I can explain what happened is that there was a door in your results that remained closed, to both you and your ob-gyn," K said. "When you did the NIPT, you didn't specifically elect to know information about your baby's sex chromosomes— this information is optional. Without your asking for it, your obstetrician could not have found it out herself. Now that I have a reason to look, I'm asking if I can open that closed door."

I'd never, ever been asked if I wanted to see information about Simone's sex chromosomes. I had never heard of Turner syndrome or monosomy X, let alone declined to find out if she had it. I'd explicitly elected to screen for chromosomal abnormalities that included a bunch of things I'd never heard of, but somehow this did not constitute electing to screen for another thing I'd never heard of.

I gave K the permission and we said we'd see each other tomorrow.

"So our baby could be shorter than the rest of the family," Gabe said to the room, the optimism palpable in his cadence. The Bumps are inordinately tall. "In our case that means she'll only be six feet."

The next day it was pouring rain, and I woke up and had a large bowl of yogurt with fresh strawberries that one of Gabe's coworkers had dropped off on our porch with ice cream the night before, along with a note that wished for each of us above all "a resilient heart."

I'd been told to come full, as the day would be a long one. Since I'd spent the previous day booking not one but two fetal diagnostic appointments—at Duke on Wednesday, at CHOP on Thursday—we were packed to go straight from this hospital to the airport. It wouldn't hurt to get a second opinion, we all agreed, and CHOP had been so great to fit me in out of nowhere, thanks to Katharine. Jamie texted to let me know he could come that night, and in the mayhem of patient portals I'd forgotten all about having asked him to come down the night before, which was by then seven hundred years ago. He was so ready to drop everything and be by my side, and that made me want to cry again. But since I didn't know where I'd be sleeping that night, I told him to stay at home.

Mom, Tom, and I sat in silence at the dining table ready to go. It was too early to leave. Mom and Tom seemed not to know what to say to me. Gabe had gone to the Quaker house he'd been going to every Sunday morning since I'd gotten pregnant, maybe a little bit before. The meetings involved sitting in silence for an hour, during which attendees could feel free to stand and speak, but no one was obligated to, and mostly no one did. Gabe often saw the same elderly couple who knew his wife was pregnant.

The Quaker house was not open on Wednesdays, but he'd called the woman who ran the meetings and told her there'd been an emergency, could he come in for just a little while today? This woman had driven to the meeting house herself, on an off day, to open the doors for him.

She'd hugged him and asked him if he wanted company. He said no, and she left him alone in the small house, where no one heard him sobbing.

He came back home at the time that he'd said he would, we packed Tom's rental car, and we left.

Driving to the hospital, Tom and Gabe in the front seat and Mom and me in the back, someone brought up *The New Naturals*, Gabe's second novel, which would be coming out that November. I'd first read the book as a Word document before I met Gabe; he'd emailed it to me when I was in LA, prefaced that it was "weirder" than his first one, that it featured a "giant baby."

This giant baby, a girl named Drop, belongs to a young couple, Rio and Gibraltar, frustrated academics in Western Massachusetts. It is not a spoiler to reveal that in the first chapter of the book, Drop is born, and then she dies. Her death—she is just days old when she begins coughing—motivates the young couple to leave their jobs and found an underground utopia. It is also not a spoiler to reveal that the utopia doesn't work. An infant dies, and society, the world, for better or worse, remains the same. It doesn't learn from its mistakes, it doesn't implode, it doesn't even bat an eye.

I'd forgotten until that moment in the rental car that my

husband had somehow prewritten our story before it'd begun, before we'd even met. I thought of Drop, growing and growing in Rio's womb and in her mind, too big for human stuff like chairs and elevators, too big for this world. I thought of Drop splashing in the waterfall and cried. Drop's death makes the book beautiful. Not so with Simone's and real life. Stuff like this, tragedy without a bottom, makes more sense in fiction than in fact.

"Fulminant hydrops," Doctor H, a maternal-fetal medicine specialist at Duke Hospital, said to us a few hours later. She had short hair and long legs and told me she too was from New York. Our parents lived one block away from each other.

We were all seated around a round wooden table in a cramped little meeting room down the hall from the room where, thirty minutes earlier, a new sonographer, this one young and cool and impossibly kind, answered every question I had. "That's not normal, is it?" I'd asked about the immense swaths of black surrounding Simone's head, the back of her neck, her spine, inside her abdomen. "No, it's not," the woman said softly but definitively, her fingers typing quickly on the keypad, taking photos and labeling them things like "heart" and "left leg" and "genital area."

Simone's heart was still beating, and when we saw her hand again, it filled me once more with a profound peace, made me want to reach inside the unknowable caves of my body and hold it. The hand wasn't moving this time; maybe she was asleep, or maybe the swelling had gotten worse since Monday. Simone's legs, the sonographer noted, were folded loosely in front of her, like she was standing up from sitting cross-legged on the floor or folding her ankles while seated in a low chair. "A real lady," the sonographer said.

Lying once again on a papered exam table with my pants rolled down, I'd asked if she knew whether Simone was in any pain, or experiencing any kind of discomfort. She turned her head from the machine and said to me with great intention and care: "Definitely not. I promise you, beyond a shadow of a doubt." I thanked her and cried. She turned back to the screen and continued her typing. "If anything," she added, "she's even more comfortable. The fluid is giving her a little extra padding."

An hour later, K and Doctor H were explaining the results of this scan to me, Gabe, and our parents. Doctor H confirmed my OB's findings from Monday: There was swelling everywhere, in the baby's abdomen and around her heart, in her skin, a massive "cystic hygroma"—until I read the full written report weeks later, I'd thought the word she said was "hydroma"—extending from the top of her head down to the bottom of her spine.

"A detailed exam was performed for the indication of concern for cystic hygroma and fetal hydrops on outside ultrasound," the report continued, "cffDNA positive for monosomy X.

"On today's ultrasound there is:

1. Large septated cystic hygroma extending from the top of the fetal head to the sacral spine
2. Bilateral pleural effusions
3. Abdominal ascites
4. Significant scalp and skin edema

5. Bilateral hydronephrosis with the maximum
   AP diameter of the left kidney measuring
   7.2 mm and the right kidney measuring
   7.5 mm. There is fluid noted in the calyces."

What's not in the report is that K, who was the only person standing in that cramped room that didn't have enough chairs for us and our parents, asked whether we'd given our baby a name yet. I told her.

"Simone," she repeated. "That's beautiful. That's what we will call her."

Nowhere on the report does it say that I asked if I could go to the bathroom, like this was a kindergarten classroom.

I came back, and Doctor H continued. "I was just explaining to your family that we don't yet know the specific cause of Simone's hydrops because the fluid is obstructing an accurate picture of her organs."

K asked if there were questions so far. She'd told me on the phone the day before to write down any questions that came to me. I still have this list in my notes app: "Can I carry her until viable outside the womb and then operate to fix this?"; "Can we drain the fluid?"; "Is this the result of something Gabe and I are carriers for?"; "Is this dangerous to my health?"; "Can I hold her?"

I told K I had one thousand.

She said that was okay.

I asked if we could drain the fluid. "Well, technically, yes, but that would not cure the pathology. The fluid would just come back." I asked if I delivered Simone now, at twenty-one weeks, could a neonatology unit save her? "Before twenty-four weeks, an otherwise healthy baby has a less than seven percent survival rate. With this much swelling and the organ failure it indicates, her chances of making it would be far lower than that." I asked, Is this something I did? They both said no.

K told us that as she'd suspected, the NIPT results she'd looked at did show indicators for Turner syndrome. "Turner is genetic, but it's not inherited," she said. Neither Gabe nor I could have been carriers for this. It was determined at random from the moment of conception; instead of twenty-three pairs of chromosomes, Simone had twenty-two pairs and one single X chromosome.

I now had to make a choice, the doctor said. I could continue with the pregnancy and see what happened. They'd have to monitor me closely, as it was possible I'd develop something called mirror syndrome, where the excess fluid and swelling in and around Simone's little body would start to affect my own blood and organs, possibly leading to preeclampsia, a hypertension disorder in pregnant or postpartum women that, if untreated, can cause maternal stroke and even death. If I chose this option, Doctor H said, I'd have to come back here weekly.

I asked what the chances were, in this scenario, that Simone would live.

"I can't tell you anything with certainty," she said. "I can't put a number on it. But with this much swelling at only twenty-one weeks, I would be really surprised if she were still alive at twenty-eight, let alone beyond that." She and K nodded at each other, a silent concurrence. They were putting this mildly.

The other option, Doctor H offered, was to terminate. The

thing was, I would have to leave the state to do this. North Carolina law prohibited abortion this late in gestation. "We send patients out of state all the time," Doctor H said. "We could transfer you to a hospital in Virginia, or in DC."

My mind flashed back to earlier that morning, when I was eating breakfast and my mother came downstairs to pull Gabe and Tom into a huddle, like she didn't mind my knowing that she was talking about me, but there was a reason why I could not be involved in the conversation. I heard "North Carolina," I heard "the laws," I heard "her safety."

I now know that my mother had spent the night googling my fate, that she knew the state had, since December, outlawed abortions for pregnancies beyond twenty weeks and six days. I was, in that little room at Duke Hospital, twenty weeks and five. Even if I had asked for an abortion on the spot, state law would also now require me to undergo mandatory counseling, and then a seventy-two-hour waiting period, during which I'd have a chance to, I guess, think it over before doing anything rash. In other words, as far as the North Carolina healthcare system was concerned, it was too late.

"Talk me out of it," I said out loud in the little meeting room, to this imaginary state-appointed counselor. "I will be your easiest case of the day."

To me, in that room, on that day, this option was beyond comprehension. K had asked me if there were religious or other reasons why termination should not even be on the table for me. I said there weren't, that it was all right for the option to be on the table. But I wasn't going to take it.

That day, I still believed that the so-called choice being presented to me actually was one. That all I had to do was pick the right door, and she would live.

"We don't expect you to decide right now," K said. They asked again if we had any questions, and we were all silent for a couple of minutes.

My mother spoke first. "So, if she does nothing," she clarified, "if she continues with the pregnancy, waits for Simone's life to take its natural course, my daughter could have preeclampsia."

Doctor H said yes.

"What would happen to her then?"

"The treatment for preeclampsia is delivery, even when it means the fetus will die. North Carolina does make an exception in cases where the mother's life is at risk." She said this like it was good news.

"But her life is not considered at risk now," Mom clarified. "She has to be in the early stages of a stroke to be treated here."

Unfortunately, these women said, yes.

"How will I know if I have mirror syndrome?" I asked.

"Your blood pressure will be high," Doctor H said. "I mean really high. Your hands and feet will swell. You will have a headache that is refractory to Tylenol. If you have any of these symptoms, you'll call us, and we will see you right away."

K stepped in here: "Do you know what refractory means?"

I said I assumed it meant unresponsive. It did.

What were the chances of this happening, Mom then wanted to know. Were they more like 5 percent, she asked, or 75? She'd done most of the talking in this meeting, channeling all her fear and love into a pragmatic quest for concrete information, for clarity. Though this was completely in keeping with the person I'd known all my life, that day I felt startled by my proximity to her agency, her strength. This is the most powerful expression of her maternal instinct: her supreme competence, her ability to take control of any situation, and handle it.

"I can't give you an exact number," the doctor said carefully, and I noticed the back of her neck becoming slightly red. I remembered my seventh-grade science teacher, how we'd all know when she was nervous or embarrassed or fed up with us because every visible bit of her pale skin—her neck, her arms, her face—would turn a bright, splotchy red. Maybe Doctor H had this condition also. Maybe it made her job harder; or maybe it helped her patients to know she was feeling things too. "But it's more than five, less than seventy-five."

Not that helpful, and she knew it. "Both choices are equally valid and loving in their own ways," this nervous doctor kept saying. She wanted me to make another appointment with them for the following Monday. She wouldn't be there, she said, she would be out of the country next week. I imagined her on an airplane to Europe or South America telling her partner or friend or parent about me, about how sad my case was, how hard her job could be sometimes. Her colleague so-and-so would be there, she said, and I'd be in fantastic hands.

The doctors left the room and the four of us were silent again. I got up to pee for the fourth time in this two-hour meeting.

"The patient and her family asked multiple thoughtful questions," Doctor H's report would say, "and are unsure how they would like to proceed at this time. Given the patient's gestational age, she understands that should she opt for termination, she will be referred out of state. Should she opt for expectant management, she understands that there is a significant risk of IUFD given the degree of hydrops identified." IUFD stands for intrauterine fetal demise.

The first person to speak when I returned to the hospital room was Mom, who raised the most immediate question of whether we wanted to go through with our existing plan to get a second opinion at CHOP. I'd completely forgotten we had plane tickets in a few hours, hotel rooms reserved. I was relieved when Gabe said that while he ultimately deferred to me, he personally could not see the point of driving to the airport, flying to Newark (the only flight that could get us there this late in the day), driving a rental car to Philadelphia, spending a night in a hotel and waking up at dawn just to do all of this all over again.

Instead we drove to Monuts, the café I'd last gone to on that sunny Saturday in November with Kate and her husband and daughter. Now it was four p.m. in January and pouring rain. There was no line, and the menu was limited to bakery items, grilled cheese, and tomato soup. We ordered three of each, for me, Mom, and Tom. Gabe got an everything bagel with cream cheese. We sat in a big booth, and I went to pee again.

Halfway through the meal, a young couple sat down at the next booth over, facing me. They had a young daughter, a toddler, who was standing on her seat and bouncing her legs jerkily, like she was trying to jump but couldn't manage to get off the ground. She had blond curly hair and threw pieces of her donut onto the ground. We all agreed not to talk about the decision we had to make until later. We needed a break from thinking.

That evening Mom and Tom and I started one of the like ten

jigsaw puzzles we would complete over the next several weeks together. I broke the moratorium and said I wanted to wait and see what happened to Simone. She wasn't dead yet, and I couldn't kill her. I'd buy a heart rate monitor at CVS and see the Duke specialists every week. I couldn't live with any decision besides this one, I said. If anyone disagreed at this point, no one said so. We ordered Thai food.

Later that night Mom went upstairs, I assumed to call work or my grandmother or something. She came back down a little bit later, in tears. Gabe went to her and hugged her.

"I'm not neutral here," she said to him through heaving sobs. "Lauren is *my* baby; I cannot lose her too." The sad, imperfect symmetry of our motherhoods; our desperation to save each of our daughters from "demise." I felt a pang of jealousy that she had a daughter who could still live.

On Thursday I felt dizzy and fell asleep for two hours in the afternoon. When I woke up, I was anxious about dying, so we took my blood pressure. It was 98 over 54. Gabe tried his: 149 over 80something—if this had been my reading, we'd have driven directly to the hospital. Mom took the machine from him; hers was even higher. Despite the medicine Tom was taking for his blood pressure, his too was alarmingly high. I said, "Seems like you guys all have mirror syndrome."

Mom was planning to leave on Saturday to go back to New York. Ever since Gong Gong died, Poh Poh had been laser-focused on his upcoming memorial, a banquet lunch on February 12 at the same Chinese restaurant in Newton, Massachusetts, where we had celebrated his ninetieth birthday in 2018. She was very concerned with getting her hair cut beforehand, as she'd be seeing a hundred people she hadn't seen since before COVID and she "looked terrible." She couldn't get to the salon on her own, so Mom had to go back to take her. Then, on Sunday, Mom was going to fly to London for a board meeting in which the large consumer goods company would announce the hiring of their new CEO. Apparently Mom would have to be there for this. Apparently this would have a significant impact on the share price, even on the stock market? I could not have cared less.

She knew I didn't want her to leave. She knew I was afraid, and I knew she was too. At one point Tom and I, doing a puzzle at the dining table, heard her arguing on the phone upstairs, in a tone she reserved only for her professional life. Hearing her sternness, her bluntness with people she works with, is always disorienting, but it also makes me feel proud. She's decisive and articulate and loud, though never disrespecting, and I always feel in my bones that she is right.

She came downstairs and Tom asked her what was wrong. She explained the crisis, and I promised her I would not repeat it here. Tom seemed to take in the situation with gravity and concern. Still unable to make myself care, I ungenerously told my father-in-law that from where I sat, there has never not been a corporate crisis it fell only on my mother to fix.

I asked Mom to please not go to London. I told her I needed her there with me. What if I got preeclampsia? What if I went into labor? What if Simone died inside me and I bled her out on my bathroom floor? What if I threw up? What if I just needed my mom?

She didn't say she would stay; she said, "We'll see." I asked her to explain to me why it was so important that she leave me to do this. The fact that I don't remember her response maybe means she didn't have a good one, or maybe it means I am bad at listening. She said, "I'll see if I can Zoom in for a meeting." She said,

"I won't know until Monday. You have to wait until Monday."
On top of everything else I was waiting to happen, I worried
too that she wouldn't be there to see me through it.

Of course I knew that I was being a baby; of course I knew
that in a very real way, I did not truly *need* her to hold my hand
through whatever came next. I was old enough to take care of
myself. I had a job that gave me health insurance and a husband
who wouldn't leave my side. Whatever I would need in the coming days and weeks—a doctor, anesthesia, grief counseling—she
could not have given me. Love and longing make no room for
logic. My need for my mother felt as mighty as my need for my
motherhood, for my daughter.

I waited to find out what would happen and whether she
would be there for it. I went upstairs to ride the Peloton. The
instructor, a man around my age who had no children, said we
were "going to crank up the slut," and it made me feel 1 percent
better. I heard a noise downstairs, over my headphones, a deep,
pulsing wail. I got off the bike and went downstairs.

Gabe was on a chair in the dining room, folded over, his hands
clasped behind his head. Tom was sitting on another chair at
the table, looking down into his lap. Mom was standing behind
Gabe, rubbing his back. The noise was coming from him, and I
could see every sob begin from somewhere down in his back,
thrusting upward, his anguish fighting its way out into the realm
of the living.

I don't remember what I did, whether I went to him and hugged
him, whether I just stood there, what I said, or to whom. I remember what he looked like, which was broken. I remember

thinking that to lose Simone was to grieve twice, for my child and for her other parent, the part of him that would die with her too.

Afterward, when we were alone, Mom told me I was lucky to have Gabe. I told her, not defensively, that I knew I was. She told me that when she'd lost the baby before me—this was what we always called that child, the rare times we talked about him—my father had felt sad for her, had taken care of her, but that he "didn't really get it." That they'd planned a vacation to Hawaii shortly after, with my dad's friend and his wife, who was at the time pregnant with her second child. That Mom had told my dad she didn't want to go, but he did, so they went.

I'd nearly forgotten, all these days, in my delirious solipsism, that my own mother had lost an unborn child too, also in the second trimester. I felt like I'd always known this, it was no revelation, but I'd also known the sweet, consoling narrative she couched the story in, which was that if she hadn't lost that baby, her first son, she would not have had me. "I couldn't imagine not having you," she'd say. (Maybe she would have had a second child, but genetically, timing-wise, it could not have been me.)

The story had always made me sad, but I'd also felt like I'd been my mother's reward for going through something so devastating. She often said things that were beyond our control were simply "meant to be" or else weren't. She knew I hated when she said this, and she didn't say it when Simone died. I realized maybe she'd never believed it at all, but that she'd had to keep going somehow. I didn't want to keep going, didn't want to ever love another child the way she loved me.

That night, before I went to bed, Poh Poh texted me. (The woman is a total beast on iMessage.) "Dearest Lauren, I know how hard it is to make your decision but we all know that it is the only choice going forward. All the love surrounding you will carry you through this dark hour and you will emerge so much stronger than before. I am glad you will be coming back to New York. It is very cold here be sure to have warm clothes. And I worry that your mom left for NC with a thin jacket. Lend her a sweater for the airplane coming home. I don't want her to get sick before London. Sending you all my love and hugs and prayers. Can't wait till I can hold you in my arms ❤️❤️❤️❤️❤️❤️❤️❤️❤️❤️❤️❤️❤️❤️ Poh Poh."

I went into my bedroom, closed the door, and called her. I told her I hadn't decided to come to New York yet; that a mother couldn't just give up on her child. I told her I was choosing Simone's life over mine.

With the clarity afforded to her by old age and her own fresh grief, Poh Poh was the first to knock sense into me before I was ready. "It's not giving up," she said. "You're not being logical, it's understandable right now. But listen to me: She is dying either way. The choice is not between her life and yours. The choice is between her dying and both of you dying. It is not really any choice at all."

I didn't say anything. She said, "We need you to live. Come home."

The next morning, Friday, I woke up feeling a rush of adrenaline. Gabe has told me in the past that even on normal mornings, I "wake up midsentence"; it was never truer than that day.

I was going to send emails, find doctors, find answers, make moves. "I'm hearing a lot of momentum," Natalie said when she called. "Let's go with it."

I knew Doctor H was away, so I tried to reach K, but she was busy, so instead I spoke to a kind and helpful male obstetrician on call who confirmed with me that he had my permission to contact Mount Sinai hospital in New York, to transfer my care there for a dilation and evacuation procedure, or a D&E, a surgical method for terminating second-trimester pregnancies.

I thanked him and waited, stared at my phone, willed it to ring, worked on the puzzle, ate a BLT, waited. I did not hear from Mount Sinai.

My mother made dinner for the four of us that night: pineapple chicken from Ayesha Curry's cookbook, her favorite. Until the pandemic, I'd only ever seen my mother make scrambled eggs and, when I was little, Kraft macaroni and cheese. This chicken was a new staple of hers, and watching her make it made me want to hug her and sob.

So I cannot explain or forgive myself for what happened next, though I'm honestly not sure she even remembers. When I went to walk Q, I passed through the kitchen and saw my mother standing over the counter, grating a whole piece of ginger into a small bowl, peel and all. I panicked, told her this wasn't how it worked, that I couldn't believe she didn't know to peel ginger. (I was, you may already know, incorrect. My grandmother always peeled ginger, and that's how she taught me to do it, and so I'd always believed it to be a rule. After googling it just now, I learned the peel is absolutely safe to eat, like the skin of a potato. My grandmother, for the record, also peels apples and grapes.)

Even if I had been correct, why, on this day of all days, did I choose to make her feel like an idiot, in front of my husband and father-in-law, who—bless his heart—stepped in to tell her, "I would have done the exact same thing"?

"Oh, okay," she said, "sorry. I didn't know. Where is your peeler?" I told her I would cook, just let me cook, I've got it. She said she knew how to do it, and that she wanted to make this dinner for me. I felt my face get hot, felt it might continue to boil until it exploded. I told her I was sorry, told her I was terrible, that I appreciated her cooking and that I had to take Q for a walk before dinner. I got my coat and the leash and left.

It was around five p.m. and campus was cold and dark. Q and Simone and I traced our usual route down the hill, past the sorority and then the fraternity houses, past the bell tower and Gabe's English department office, the student union and the Bojangles, the gym and the segregated cemetery and the soccer fields where students were practicing and playing Frisbee and stretching and strengthening under the bright lights.

From the sidewalk you can lean over a stone wall and look down over these fields, which is what I had done one day the previous July when Gabe had taken up soccer again, buying cleats and a ball and a small red goal with a white net and bringing these down to the fields that were empty of students in the mornings before it got too hot.

Thinking I'd see him dribbling and shooting alone that day, I'd instead found him playing a pickup game with a random assortment of people, men and women and boys and girls, all moving at different speeds and levels of agility and investment. Even at ten a.m., everyone was sweating. Gabe stuck to one side of the field, running up and down its length with his eye ever on the ball, and the few times he got it he dribbled and passed to the same man, an older stranger. I have no idea what it was about watching him that day, on that field with those strangers, that expanded my capacity for love.

Walking with Q that January, carrying the weight of Simone and my grief, I stopped and saw Gabe again, in my mind this time, wearing track pants and the big black hoodie he stole from his dad, crouching down to teach a little girl, our little girl, what to do with a soccer ball. I saw her standing there, just a toddler, bundled up like a potato because it was colder than usual for North Carolina, staring up at him with eyes that looked like his or like mine or just like her own, having no idea what the point of this game was or why he wanted her to do it, but wanting to understand, wanting to do what he did, wanting him to be happy and proud of her. Dear Simone, I wanted to tell her, her heart still beating strong and fast right beneath mine: He is.

I cried on that walk, cried for my mother and for my daughter, students passing me carrying their backpacks and takeout to the library or back to their rooms or to practice or to meet their friends. To every woman and girl I passed on any sidewalk or store aisle or hospital waiting room during that month, I'm sorry for my puffy eyes and my shameless wailing. More so, I am sorry for projecting my dead daughter's impossible future onto yours, for wondering if she'd have been like you, walked like you, smiled politely at strangers like you smiled at me, taken the classes you love, sneezed or fallen in love or worn clips in her hair the way you do.

I can live with not knowing the answers to these questions, I really can. What I cannot abide is that she will not know them either. I know that she was only mine to protect, but not truly mine; her life would have been hers to do with what she pleased; my only role would have been to support. It is one more cruelty that this cruel death has been the thing to convince me that at the bottom of the ledger, when all is added and subtracted, life is a good thing, and that to not experience it is a tragedy. But no, the world is neither cruel nor merciful, it just is.

Little one, I'm sorry for my sudden, incessant, heaving sobs that no doubt woke you from gentle sleep throughout those heinous days, nine days that changed me more than the previous thirty-three years had combined. They were not all tears of sadness. These were our last days together, the end of our life as one body, and I knew that, and enshrined it in my soul. If I could have done it all over again, I wouldn't have changed a thing.

I got back and the house smelled sweet and warm, and the table was set. Someone had bought wine, and I asked if they thought I could have a glass. "I think it's okay," Tom said, and I laughed a little.

We ate around the table and all marveled at how delicious the chicken was. That night I fell asleep quickly but woke up at two or three a.m., my heart racing. I checked my hands, were they swollen? My wedding band felt tight. I nudged Gabe awake, terrified. "Do my hands look swollen to you?" I asked. He turned his light on and said, "I don't think so." He held each of my hands and said, "No, I've held your hands so many times. They feel the same as always."

When I woke up again, it was morning, and I was okay. But we knew, Gabe and I, that we could not keep waiting for something to happen. In the meantime, until we heard back from Mount Sinai, we agreed we'd make some calls. I reached out to two doctors in New York whom I'd seen for years until I moved to North Carolina: my general physician and the gynecologist she'd referred me to in 2018, a pelvic surgeon and oncologist named Doctor P, who had long, straight gray hair and wore giant glasses and black leather skirts to give me a Pap smear. I admired these women, wanted to emulate them, most importantly trusted them with my life.

I did not know how far I'd get on a Saturday, but minutes after giving a breathless and scrambled summary of what was happening to Doctor P's receptionist ("I know she's not an obstetrician," I said, "but I need a referral, my baby is dying"), the doctor was calling me from her cell phone.

Without panic or pleasantry, Doctor P did not skip a beat. There was an obstetrician in maternal-fetal medicine at Lenox Hill named Doctor B. No further questions, he was my guy. "Tell him I sent you," she said. On the hospital website, he looked about thirteen. "It's probably an old picture," Tom said.

Jamie's father, my former stepfather, happens to be on the board of the healthcare network that owns Lenox Hill. He'd known what was happening, so I called him, and an hour later Doctor B had called me from his cell phone, and was now explaining to me with care and compassion and a thick Israeli accent what my options were, as he saw them.

"I do not in any way want to influence your decision to terminate or not terminate," he said, and I wondered how many times he had had to have this delicate conversation in his career. He did not sound thirteen.

"If you come to see me, we will do our own ultrasound to confirm your current doctors' findings. Assuming we do find that the hydrops is as severe as you're describing, I am afraid your baby will not survive, and—I'm sorry to put this so bluntly— the longer it takes her to pass, the greater the risk to your body. So, I'd like to know from you what you intend to do in that case."

The doctor said this all over speakerphone; I was sitting at our round wooden dining table with my mother and father-in-law, the Frank Lloyd Wright puzzle I'd bought when we visited Gabe's family in Chicago half-finished in front of us. I picked up a piece and put it into place. I told him I understood, and that if there were really no possibility of my baby surviving, I would accept the need to terminate.

To my horror, the decisions were not over. Termination could look one of two ways, he explained. The D&E the Duke doctors had described would involve a number of tools inserted into my uterus to, well, evacuate my child. Though these tools presented a small chance of damaging the uterine lining, he said, the real reason he discouraged me from choosing this option was because of Simone's size. Though I was only five months along, the swelling could mean she was the size of a twenty-six-week fetus. "I don't want to be too graphic," he said slowly, "but with this method, your baby would not come out in one piece."

There was another, much better option, he said calmly. Assuming Simone was still alive by the time I came to New York, he first would insert a tiny needle through my abdomen into her heart, to stop it. After that, an obstetrician would induce labor, and I would deliver the baby vaginally. If all went well, the procedure would require minimal instruments, and I could hold her afterward.

"To me, this is the most humane way," he said, and I trusted him.

I asked him about the timeline. Gabe has described his feeling in those days as a bomb waiting to go off inside me but the bomb was our daughter. Could I wait until Thursday, Mom mouthed for me to ask. Wednesday was when she would be flying back from London. He did not know that the reason I asked him if I could wait until Thursday was to work the death of my daughter around the British company's public relations schedule.

He said that would not be advisable in the event that I had to stay in the hospital longer than a day, which wasn't unlikely. "Hospital staff is reduced on the weekends," he said. "If you can avoid being there past Friday, you should."

Okay, we said. Tuesday. He told me to text or call him if I had any other questions until then. I thanked him and hung up.

The next day, Jamie called me. Jamie never called me.

"Yo," he said.

"Hi," I said.

"What's up?" he said.

It was the first time I'd smiled in days. What was up.

"Just sitting here with Mom and Tom doing a puzzle," I said. We'd actually just finished the Frank Lloyd Wright one, and Tom was meticulously breaking apart every single piece before putting them back into the box—a role he took upon himself ever since I'd mentioned, offhandedly, that I hated starting a puzzle and finding pieces already attached.

"Tom's there?" he said. "Tell him yo."

I did. Tom smiled his wide, gentle smile, the one Gabe sometimes makes too.

"What are you up to?" I asked. I thought about the last time
we'd spoken, how little I'd known then, how desperate my voice
must have sounded.

"I got groceries, we're making dinner tonight. Junior got a
fish." His roommate.

We talked about nothing for like ten more minutes. We didn't
mention Simone or doctors or abortions; he only told me stupid
things his roommates had done, stupid jokes like the ones he
used to tell when we were younger, when he'd respond to my
panic attacks not by coddling me but by snapping me out of it,
reminding me that there are worlds beyond my fear, and they are
mostly boring. When we finally hung up, Mom was looking at
me as if to ask what just happened. This was the best way he
knew to show me he loved me, to show me he was there for me.
The next day he did the same thing with Gabe.

Mom made no big announcement when she decided not to go
to London, when she told them she'd not be leaving the country
for the sake of being in the hospital when her daughter's daughter died, and then was born. If the stock market collapsed, I
didn't feel it. What I did feel was a surge of pure, unadulterated
relief, a little residual annoyance, and a great deal of gratitude. I
needed my mother, and she would stay.

That Sunday, before we left for New York, Gabe and Hopscotch and Q and Mom and Tom and I went on a hike through
the Carolina North Forest. Hopscotch walked up ahead, peeing
in small amounts every few steps, pausing to look back to make

sure we were all following, to make sure his pack was intact. Gabe had a little case of treats strapped around his waist, and he doled them out to Hop when another dog passed, training him not to jump or freak out. It was forty degrees, and I lent Mom my mittens, because pregnancy had helped my circulation so much that my hands and feet were perfectly warm without them.

We got back to the car and I crouched down to hug Hopscotch on the pavement, feeling a wave of sadness as I said goodbye to him before Gabe took him to board for two weeks. We were bringing Q to New York with us, because she was small and could handle the nine-hour car ride and my mom's apartment, where she'd spent so much time the first years of her life. Hopscotch was still a baby, and sometimes a single car on the street could send him into a full panic. He'd never left North Carolina, and was already forty pounds and unpredictable. It would be better for him to hang out with the friends he saw at daycare every day. I still felt like I was abandoning him.

That night, Tom drove Mom and me to RDU in his rental car, and we three boarded an airport shuttle from the rental car return to our gates. Tom got off the shuttle first, to fly home to Chicago; Mom and I got off next at Terminal 2. On the bus I cried softly but visibly, and Tom put his arm around my shoulder. We hugged tearfully in front of the other travelers, who looked tired and disgruntled.

Mom and I were early for our flight, and I was hungry, so we sat down at an airport café and ordered greasy flatbreads heaped with melted cheese. I cried there too, less softly, and Mom held both of my oily hands in hers across the small table. "I don't want to do this," I said.

She looked at me, at the gate at RDU, like her life was only me. She squeezed my hands tighter. "This is important," she said. "When you are ready to hear this, I want you to try to focus not on mourning your motherhood. It is not your motherhood that you've lost. You're mourning Simone, just Simone."

When I walked into my childhood bedroom around ten that night, there was a Valentine's Day drugstore cookie on my nightstand, shaped like a bear holding a heart that said LOVE on it, on top of a card that said "Laur" in Caroline's handwriting. She and Jamie had been over for an early dinner that night with Poh Poh, who'd sent everyone home before Mom and I got there so she could go to sleep.

There was also a log from the living room fireplace on my desk. "After I put the cookie in there Jamie said he was going to leave something for you too," Caroline said when I texted her, and I pictured him looking around for the most random object in the house to gift me as a weird and childish way to make me smile, which it did.

Alone for the first time in days, in the dark, quiet room where I had fallen asleep so many times before, surrounded by the family and the walls and the smells and the city sounds that had comforted me all my life, I thought about what I was about to do, and the other faceless women who had endured or would endure the same before and after me. I wondered how much harder this already intolerable situation could have been without the money and access I had but had not earned, their power to smooth over all the logistical friction that compounds medical tragedies like mine.

What if I hadn't had such deep roots in a state that could treat me? Or the means to get there, or the arms reaching out to console me when I arrived? Would I still be an anonymous diagnosis sitting in a fax machine somewhere in Virginia or DC? If I made it to one of those unfamiliar places, who would care about me when I got there?

I don't know how I slept at all that night, but when I woke up on Monday the weather was sunny and brisk; even though it was only the end of January, it was the kind of day that tricks you into thinking spring might be around the corner. I went for a walk around the Central Park Reservoir, a walk I'd done so many times in my life, as a kid after school; as an adult jogging on cold, dark mornings; as a pregnant person, only weeks earlier, walking with my brother and cousins as we grieved our grandfather.

I saw a group of tiny girls wearing the uniform I had as a child, obviously students at the school I attended, no older than kindergarten, being corralled by two or three teachers into formation against the iron railing that separated the dirt path from the water below.

As I passed them I got a call from a North Carolina number. It was K, the genetic counselor at Duke. Since I hadn't heard back from Mount Sinai over the weekend, I'd forgotten to let her know I'd made my own plan of care in New York. She asked the name of the doctor I'd be seeing, and I gave it to her. She said she would reach out to him directly, to communicate with him about my treatment, about his findings, about confirming the Turner diagnosis. She said she wanted to rule out blood disorders in Gabe and me. She said something about a condition common in Southeast Asians, which neither of us are. I thanked her, hung up, and turned off the path toward the park's Eighty-Fifth Street exit.

Natalie came over that afternoon. We sat with Mom around the kitchen table and talked loudly and emotionally, like we weren't already long depleted from talking, like we could talk like this for days. One of us remembered out loud that just six weeks earlier, at our wedding, Baldwin had sat around this same table in his velvet blazer eating catered cookies on a literal silver platter. That had been another life.

Gabe and Q arrived around three, and by some miracle they found a parking space right in front of the awning of our building. He could stay there indefinitely as long as he just sat in it for an hour and a half on Monday and Thursday mornings when the traffic police came.

We ordered takeout, the four of us, pizzas and pastas and a salad with Gorgonzola that I didn't bother to make sure was pasteurized. After one day at work in Chicago, Tom decided he couldn't stay away and flew to meet us again in New York. Mom made up a bed for him on the enormous green velvet couch in the upstairs TV room. I have no memory of going to sleep that night; it amazes me now that I was able to sleep at all.

In the morning I put on old leggings and Gabe's soft black T-shirt and a fleece jacket and went downstairs to eat a bowl of oatmeal. We hugged Tom goodbye and Mom and Gabe and I took a short cab ride to the office of the obstetrician Doctor B had selected for me, Doctor R.

Outside of the office, a brass plaque told me this obstetrician shared a practice with a gynecologist who happened to be the mom of a friend I hadn't seen in years. She would never know me, but still I imagined her telling him she'd seen me that day, how miserable I looked. I imagined them both feeling sorry for me.

I could see the face of the only other woman in the waiting room register my sadness, wonder why I was rolling so deep at the gynecologist's office at eight a.m. Christmas cards bearing faces of babies and children of all ages covered the façade of the half wall that separated the waiting room from the receptionist's desk. I told this receptionist my name and she gave me a thick pile of forms to fill out. Mom, Gabe, and I took up basically the entire tiny waiting room.

Doctor R, a thin, dark-haired woman in a crisp white Oxford shirt and black slacks, came out to greet me. We shook hands, and she ushered Mom and Gabe and me into her office, an elegant mahogany setup that barely fit the four of us. She sat at her computer and asked me questions about my medical history and what my pregnancy had been like until that point. She asked how long we'd been trying to get pregnant before Simone and we told her it had been the second month I was off birth control. She told me I would have a family one day. I couldn't say how far that was from what I wanted to hear, so instead I wept.

She gave me a quick manual vaginal exam in the next room, and then when we rejoined my mom and husband in her office, she gave us a run-through of everything that was going to happen. Her plan was to do everything possible to avoid surgical intervention. She would be giving me medicine to induce labor, monitoring my cervix as it dilated, and proceeding with a vaginal delivery. She said they'd give me a higher-than-normal dose of the epidural whenever I wanted it, since there was no danger of the anesthetic harming the baby.

My mom asked how she would make sure that "everything came out," meaning the placenta and whatever other tissue has to be expelled in childbirth besides the actual child. Doctor R replied that worst case, if the placenta did not release as it was supposed to, it was possible to then do a D&E to remove it. Depending on how labor went, a C-section was not out of the question, though she understood we all wanted that to be a last resort.

I thanked her and we walked the few blocks up Lexington to Lenox Hill. We took the elevator to the maternal-fetal medicine floor, where we sat in a sterile gray waiting room on chairs separated by clear COVID-era partitions. There were several other women and couples in the waiting room; some were asked if they wanted to schedule follow-up appointments as they left, and I briefly hated them. A thin man stood next to his seated wife, who looked about as pregnant as I was and was also filling out forms. From the look on his face, I could tell they were there for different reasons, for normal reasons, hopeful, anticipatory ones.

Mom had been sitting across from Gabe and me, but when she saw me start to cry, she got up from her seat and knelt on the floor in front of mine, hands gripping my lap. I told her I didn't want to make a scene, freak everybody else out, the women in the waiting room, remind them how fragile their happiness was. Maybe they already knew.

The first person to greet us there was not Doctor B, but a petite woman who looked around fifty and was dressed in regular clothes, not scrubs. She introduced herself as a "nurse navigator," which was something I hadn't heard of. She said she would be taking care of me from now until I left the hospital. Anything I needed, any question I had, I should reach out to her. Here was her cell phone number. She had a raspy Midwestern accent and asked if we were Carolina fans, because Gabe was wearing the light blue hat he always wore. He told her yes, but that he was originally from Chicago. "I'm from Michigan," she said. "State fan." She smiled a huge smile and said, "We have a lot of class, all of it low," and laughed at herself.

Soon Doctor B appeared, a tall and wiry man with curly blond hair flecked with gray, wearing a checkered button-down shirt and khakis. His hand, when I shook it, was bony and warm. He guided the three of us to a narrow exam room where a middle-aged sonographer with a foreign accent I couldn't place moved another wand over my belly gently but intentionally, with the ease of someone who'd had decades of practice. There was a younger man standing behind her, looking over her shoulder, whispering clipped, staccato words I couldn't decipher. He never introduced himself or said a word to me. I made awkward eye contact with him again and again and fought the urge to ask him to leave.

As we beheld the ultrasound outline of our daughter for the third time in eight days, this time our eyes were trained enough to see for ourselves that the swelling had gotten worse. Her hand no longer moved, and the black was everywhere. Still, we could see her face, her tiny nose, her still-crisscrossed legs. She'd fought like hell for every day she got to live inside me, fought harder than any child or adult should have to. She wouldn't have to fight anymore.

Doctor B came in, studied the screen, and confirmed Duke's diagnosis. He came over to the left side of the table I was lying on and reiterated that he thought the safest and most humane course of treatment would be to administer the solution he'd talked about, through a needle inserted directly through my belly and uterus and into her heart. I still had a chance to change my mind. He asked if we needed a minute to think. I said nothing. Gabe said yes.

Everyone filed out of the room, including my mom. Someone asked if we wanted the lights back on (they'd been off for the sonogram), and we said no. Before she left, the sonographer held my hand, looked into my eyes, and assured me that there was no chance for my child to live. She told me she felt sad, but also hopeful for us. I thanked her.

The door closed and it was just Gabe and Simone and me in the dark. I don't remember what we said. I remember that I cried. I remember that Gabe cried too. I remember that we hugged kind of sideways, our cheeks touching, his head and shoulders shielding my eyes from the thin bright light of Seventy-Seventh Street filtering in from the window behind me.

Someone knocked on the door. It was the nurse navigator. She asked if she could come in. We said yes. She stood in the doorway and she was holding our backpacks. I'd forgotten we had backpacks. She asked, gently, if we'd decided. I nodded and told her we were ready to do the procedure. I pray this forever remains the worst moment of my life.

Mom came back in and hugged both of us. She told me she loved me with her whole heart, something she'd said since I was little.

Gabe sat back down in his chair to my left, behind me so I had to look up and back to see him. Doctor B came in and narrated every action he took. He rubbed an antibiotic on my abdomen that dyed my skin a dark orange. He prepared a silver tray of needles. The first, he said, was smaller; it would just take a sample of the amniotic fluid surrounding Simone to confirm her Turner syndrome.

The second needle was thicker. I wished it would hurt me more. It contained the chemical that would end Simone's short life. He inserted it and explained that he had to leave it inside me for a little bit, while he watched on the ultrasound monitor to make sure the flicker of her heart had stopped.

I looked toward the screen and saw my daughter alive for the last time. The tiny, powerful heartbeat that had weathered the impossible and kept on going, determined to live. The heartbeat that had over the past five months reassured me not just of her own vitality, but of mine. I couldn't bear to see it stilled.

"Look at me," Gabe said, gripping both of my hands tightly over my head as I wept, our faces inches from each other and divided by two blue disposable masks, the eyes above his wet and red. I imagined Doctor B and the sonographer staring at the screen as intensely as Gabe and I stared at each other, all of us waiting.

"It's okay," Gabe said so many times, even though everyone in that room knew it wasn't. "Just look at me. It's okay. I love you."

I can talk about everything else that's happened, with an urgency to tell anyone who will listen about Simone, who she was, what happened to her, that she existed. This moment is the one I can't access myself, let alone repeat.

It was around eleven a.m. on January 31, and I was alone in my body again. Simone was dead; now she had to be born.

She started up again, cold and trembling
with the shock: for a moment she seemed to have lost
her hold of the child. But no—she was mistaken—the
tender pressure of its body was still close to hers: the
recovered warmth flowed through her once more,
she yielded to it, sank into it, and slept.

—Edith Wharton, *The House of Mirth*

After that, we had bagels. I'd learned I wouldn't be allowed to eat once I got to the labor and delivery floor, and I am embarrassed to report that I was starving. Gabe went across the street to Pick A Bagel and got me a sesame with butter, and everything and whole wheat with cream cheese for himself and my mom. Doctor B heard about the bagels and said we could eat them in his office. I sat in his chair with my mom and husband across from me, as if they were my patients. I found a pen and wrote the doctor a note on a Post-it, thanking him for taking care of me and my daughter. My hand was shaking. The bagel was fucking delicious. We cleaned up the crumbs and followed the nurse navigator to another floor.

We were led through a hallway lined with professional portraits of multiracial babies to a room with mahogany walls and two hospital beds in it, facing each other, divided by a wall that could slide open and shut. I assumed someone else would be occupying the other bed, but was told they were both ours. "So Gabe or Mom can get some sleep while we wait," the nurse said, smiling.

This was my first hospitalization, so I had nothing to compare it to, but even so I suspected this setup was much nicer than normal. I changed into a comfortable gown and got settled. Gabe took the chair to the right of my bed, up against the window. He put his iPad on the table in front of us and put on the first episode of *Veep*.

Doctor B had told me to expect the labor induction and delivery to take at least a day altogether, maybe two, depending on how my body responded to the drugs that would stimulate contractions. The first couple of hours in that room were spent gathering signatures and administrative information, as well as tethering every part of me to some machine or other. A nurse named L introduced herself. Her name sounded Vietnamese, and her voice was soft. She handed me a little red button attached to a wire and said that if I needed anything at all, I should press that button, and she would come. Over the next twenty-four hours my mom and Gabe would have to yell at me several times to push that button, because I had such a hard time determining what constituted a suitable reason to summon help.

L strapped the armband of a heart rate monitor around my right arm and said it was going to get kind of annoying because it would stay on all day and all night until this baby came out of me. I famously hate having my blood pressure taken. It's worse to me than getting a shot or giving blood. The throbbing vein freaks me out, and there's also something about the band constricting further and further that makes me worry it will never stop and my arm will be left permanently cinched like sausage links.

Next was the IV, which would also stay attached to me for the duration of my luxury stay. L had a hard time finding a suitable vein, so after poking several holes in my arm she called for backup. A much more gregarious red-haired nurse named D arrived and announced that she was the resident vein master. She also seemed to be the class clown of the floor, lifting spirits of patients and colleagues with her silly and self-deprecating humor, her way of making you feel like you were best friends after having known each other only fourteen seconds. D slid the long needle under the skin of my left forearm like it was nothing. She bandaged me up and told me I was good to go. She wasn't my nurse, she said, but she'd come back to check on me anyway. I could tell everyone I encountered felt bad for me, and that they were also genuinely nice people. Maybe only the nicest people got put on cases like mine.

Doctor B arrived to see how I was doing. He told us that the result of the genetic test he took from the amniotic fluid had not been successful, because there had not actually been any amniotic fluid to test. I said I didn't understand what he meant.

"The baby was so swollen," he explained, "because she had absorbed all the fluid surrounding her into her body, and her kidneys were not able to flush it out."

I said, "Oh."

He said, "There is still another way to confirm the Turner diagnosis, but it requires taking a very small piece of her skin when she is born, and doing a biopsy. Are you all right with this?"

My daughter was dead. She would be cremated upon birth. I told him I was all right with it.

It was not until three p.m. that a resident, or maybe she was an attending, anyway I never saw her again after this, gave me the first dose of Pitocin, a pill she inserted into my vagina to induce labor. I considered the literalness of what was happening to my body. It thought we were still pregnant. It thought we had eighteen weeks to go. It thought we were still working hard to keep this baby in here, to keep this baby alive. It did not want to let her go.

We watched an episode of *Veep*, which Gabe kept having to get up and pause every time a nurse or resident or attending or doctor or administrative coordinator or my father-in-law came in to check on me. To check on my blood pressure, which kept dipping below 90 over 60; to change my IV bag; to bring me a Popsicle, the most I could have in my stomach in case I needed an emergency cesarean section. I was starving, and pregnancy had taught me to fear my hunger: It could roar suddenly and without warning, make me feel like an animal seeking prey. If I did not respond to it immediately, the spiral of nausea would be unending. I was afraid, even in this hospital room, even as my daughter was dead inside of me and I now had to get her out, that I might throw up.

At about five, Mom and Tom, who'd come to hang out as we waited, left to eat, which was rude. I'd felt some cramping before they went, but thirty minutes after they were gone, the pain swelled sharply and without much warning. When people say contractions feel like period cramps but worse, that is like saying being stabbed is like a worse version of a flu shot.

At once piercing and diffuse, as if a hand were reaching into me and wringing my insides—this is foreshadowing—every contraction made a mockery of the last. The pain abated for a minute at most before coming back for me. I have never had a "normal," non-induced labor, but apparently contractions are supposed to start spread out? Like, multiple minutes apart? Pitocin, all business, skips this runway.

In the short windows between contractions, I responded to texts from Devin, who was sending me several, helpfully diverting "who to them" lists, where I had to rank the items she gave me in order of least famous to most: "Florence Pugh; Florence, Italy; Florence and the Machine; Flo from Progressive; Flo Rida; Florence Nightingale." We agreed Italy was the biggest "them," but disagreed wildly on the rest.

Devin also texted, "This is the bravest thing that anyone I've known has ever had to do."

During the second or third contraction, when I realized through the delirium of pain what was happening to me, I finally asked for the epidural. L had asked me repeatedly, throughout the *Veep*-watching portion of the day, if I wanted the epidural as soon as induction started. I said no, because I don't know why. Something about my general disinclination toward medication and pain relief in particular? About not wanting to be paralyzed below the waist in case I had to get up to pee? A catheter hadn't sounded so appealing until I understood for the first time in my sheltered little life the upper limit of what a body could do to itself, the kind of pain that comes from nowhere but within, a guttural twisting from the very epicenter of my self, a groaning ache that was the violent culmination of all that had come before. I asked L for the epidural.

When she left to go order this, another contraction started. I clutched Gabe and asked him to call my mom. I need her to come back, I said. I'm scared. Mom and Tom came back, terrified to see me in that much pain. My teeth could not stop violently chattering. I was cold, but in a way that I had never been cold before. Cold from the inside. L said that was because of the room-temperature (not human body–temperature) IV fluid coursing through my body.

The anesthesiologist still had not come. I had waited too long—he was now administering sweet, sweet relief to someone else, someone who'd had the good sense to ask for it early. Mom and Gabe were frustrated that it was taking so long, but I had lost all concept of time. Whoever this other patient was needed it too; I could wait.

One contraction got so bad that I begged L not to leave my side until it was over. I needed her, I mean physically needed her, needed her small arms to hold mine, her masked face directly staring at my sweaty, unmasked one, to tell me I was going to get through it, to remind me to breathe, to tell me I was strong. I asked if I was hurting her and she said, "You have no idea what we have endured in here."

She said she needed to go check on the anesthesiologist. I told her I would simply not keep living if she left. She said okay. She asked if it would be okay to have D, the red-haired nurse from before, take her place until she got back. I said that would be okay, because I liked D and because I felt like I had no more chips to play after threatening my own death.

D came back, and she sat on the edge of my bed like my mom did when I was a kid, like she still does sometimes, leaning onto my legs, asking me what is wrong. D knew what was wrong. D did not seem scared. She told me that growing up, her sister had these really horrific migraines. To help her through them, D would pinch and poke and squeeze hard on other parts of her body, like her legs. This is what she did to me now. Remember "Indian rug burns"? This is what she was doing to my shins and thighs just above my knees. It hurt. Whether because the brain can only process one nexus of pain at a time, or maybe because it was just a mental distraction, I felt the slightest bit less bad.

L came back. The anesthesiologist was finishing up and he would be in soon. Okay. Another contraction was starting. Mom and Tom and Gabe were in the room too, they must have been, but for some reason I only remember these two young women, D and L, gripping random parts of my body as I gripped random parts of theirs, the strange rituals of this cadre. I told them I might have to poop. I hadn't pooped in a few days, which was not unusual throughout my second trimester. They said okay, let's go. We went. I slid the door closed but I could still hear the girls outside, talking with each other about a time they'd both had to help a patient on the toilet and ended up, all three of them, on the tile floor, in hysterics. I laughed with them. I apologized, apparently I did not have to poop.

When I got back into bed, D asked me if it had felt like I "needed to bear down." This phrase made me want to heave. "Sometimes, when the body is ready to deliver, it can feel like you just need to take a really big shit," she said. I said I did not need to bear down. What a foul business this is, having a body.

A different doctor, a quiet man whose focused restraint I found comforting in a complementary way to D's boisterous intimacy, came to check if I was crowning. He stuck his fingers inside my cervix and determined that I was, wait for it, all of one centimeter dilated. I thought about the night in the emergency room

three months earlier, how I'd thought *that* pain had been extreme. How I'd wondered if *that* were what labor might feel like.

The anesthesiologist came, with a little tray of tools he was
pushing in front of him. D and L asked my family to leave the
room, to wait outside in the hall, and then it really was just us
and the guy with the needle in the room. I had to sit up and turn
so my legs were dangling off the edge of the bed, facing the
door. The anesthesiologist wheeled his little tray to the side of
the bed facing my back, and D and L each held one of my hands,
staring into my face, reassuring me.

Another contraction started. The man was still preparing his
tools. I was sitting up, clutching these two young women for
dear life, howling. This was the worst one yet. In the throes of it,
D pulled down her mask, so I could see her full face for the first
time. She looked even younger than I had thought, and she had
freckles like mine.

"Look at me," she said. "I need you to listen very closely. Are
you listening?"

I nodded, my face still contorted, covered in sweat, tears.

"Do you know who gave birth in this exact room?"

And then I knew. The tabloids from eleven years earlier, al-
leging that the birth of Blue Ivy Carter, on January 7, 2012, had
shut down a floor of Lenox Hill's labor and delivery wing. How
excessive, these tabloids had claimed, how unfair to all the regular women who needed care on that day. One piece I had read
before going to this same labor and delivery wing quoted a Lenox
Hill representative as denying that the Carters cleared out the
rest of the wing for their peace and privacy.

D's face was inches from mine, her calm, slow breaths now mixing with my desperate ones, her eyes staring straight into my soul. She said: "It's all true."

D and L were both far too young to have been working here in 2012. But they knew. Beyoncé had delivered in the exact same place I was now in; Jay-Z had napped in the same extra bed that Gabe and my mother would take turns in that night. The contraction abated, and the anesthesiologist was ready.

I was going to feel a pinch, he said, like what you feel when you get Novocaine before having a cavity filled. I don't mind needles, never have, and this one was no different. It was what came after the pinch that still keeps me awake at night. I could not see what he was doing, but I knew there was a needle being threaded up my spine. I remember the shock like it is still happening, the jolt of lightning that radiated suddenly from my spine down my left leg to the knee, the jolt that made me flinch and cry, which in turn made the nurses yell in terror, "DO NOT MOVE. YOU HAVE A NEEDLE IN YOUR SPINE. ONE CENTIMETER IN THE WRONG DIRECTION AND YOU COULD BE PARALYZED."

This was pain, this was fear. He finished, and I was okay. D and L helped me lie back down, and L inserted my catheter, since I would no longer be able to get up to pee. I was handed another little button, this one I could press when I needed more anesthesia. It wouldn't let me overdose, the man said, it would automatically cap, so I didn't need to worry about pressing it too much. I thanked him and he left. The contractions were completely gone.

Gabe, Mom, and Tom came back in, in various states of distress.

They'd heard me wailing outside the room, they said. It seemed like it was taking longer than it should, they said. They loved me so much. I knew, I said, and I was okay. I loved them too.

The exact sequence of events of the rest of that night, the night of January 31 into the morning of February 1, 2023, has already blurred. Here is what I remember:

Dos Toros burritos, picked up and eaten by my bedside by my husband, mother, and father-in-law.

Being starving, wanting to eat everything, anything, being allowed only Popsicles, savoring every drop of them: raspberry, then strawberry, then another strawberry.

The blood pressure monitor squeezing my arm every few minutes, beeping, beeping, sometimes alerting L when my results were too low.

Dropping two out of the four tubs of Carmex I'd brought with me somewhere in the bed. Mom on her hands and knees on the hospital floor, searching underneath the hospital bed, finding nothing. Maybe the bed ate them. Maybe they are still there.

Saying goodbye to D at the end of her shift, her promising to come back to see me the next day; and then to L, who was off the next day. "Hopefully by my next shift, you will have gone home," she said. I told her I loved her, and I meant it. These people who shared the darkest moment of my life with me, who tended my blood and urine and brought me ginger ale and talked to me from outside the bathroom and held me as I writhed and cried—I would most likely never see them again.

Meeting W, the overnight nurse, her eyes already wet before we'd said hello to each other. W telling me, "I'm here for you."

W attaching a contraction monitor around my waist that made my stomach skin itchy.

Falling asleep, Gabe in the reclining chair to my right, telling me he loved me. Telling Mom to close her eyes in Jay-Z's bed; nothing was going to happen for a while. I promised I'd wake her up if I needed her.

Dozing in and out for a few hours, jolting awake a couple of times with that feeling like I was falling, and Gabe saying, "It's okay. You're okay."

SportsCenter playing on the TV suspended from a corner of the ceiling, basketball, LeBron on loop, how close was he to surpassing Kareem Abdul-Jabbar's something something. The balletic beauty of this game, its soothing rhythm, the back-and-forth, back-and-forth movement, the arc of the ball, and the body, in flight. This was a world untouched by physical incapacity, predicated upon its exact opposite, upon gargantuan strength that somehow also defied gravity. A game that lulled me to sleep on so many normal winter nights, Gabe lying next to me and jolting in frustration, or saying to himself, softly, "splash."

The male doctor arriving to check how dilated I was. Three centimeters. Him inserting another dose of the Pitocin, followed by a balloon—yes, a balloon—threaded through my vagina into my cervix. Him inflating the balloon. Tape, so much tape, attaching various tubes to my legs and back and stomach.

Mom getting up, Gabe taking the bed for a couple hours. Gabe asking Mom, from the vantage point of the other bed, what that number was on a monitor next to me that I couldn't see. The number kept rising and falling, between eight or ten or twelve and up to the forties, and back down again. Mom telling him that it was reading my contractions. When the number was high, I was having one. I heard that in disbelief. I couldn't have told you when I was having a contraction if you'd paid me. This epidural, so far, was a godsend.

Tiny sips of ginger ale.

At five a.m., Doctor R came in. She was wearing blue scrubs, her hair under a blue cap, a gleaming diamond chain around her neck, a simple gold wedding band around her small finger.

Doctor R said I was ready to deliver. Gabe and Mom woke up. Doctor R wheeled in several trays and a large rolling light that she couldn't figure out how to turn on. Mom or Gabe helped her. "I'm better at delivering babies than I am at figuring out lights," she said.

I didn't understand how I could possibly be "ready," because I didn't feel any different than I had before, when professionals had told me that I was absolutely not ready. I never felt the need to "bear down." My water never broke. There was no water. It was all inside of her.

Because Simone was no longer alive, she could not do her part in making her way out. (At least this is something my mom said to me at some point; I'm not sure if that is what actually happens during live births.) She was also, as we'd learned from the various ultrasounds that week, in breech position; her head was facing up toward my stomach, and her feet and butt were down toward my cervix. This was not abnormal for a baby at twenty-two weeks, when a healthy, non-swollen baby would be doing flips and turns every day, and only at thirty-six weeks would she (typically, hopefully) settle in a position to go headfirst through the birth canal.

No time for that now. The male doctor returned and said he would be assisting in the delivery. Gabe sat up in the recliner to the right of my head, holding both of my hands through her birth as he had through her death. I told him I was afraid. He told me I could do it; he would be right there. My mom sat on the other side of me a few feet away.

What followed was the realest thing I've ever experienced. "I can see her," Doctor R said as they both peered through my widened cervix, and I let out a nervous laugh. It was her, Simone, my entire heart, my whole life, she was really just in there this whole time. I cannot explain how or why a part of me, throughout the time we spent in this hospital room, kind of forgot she was dead. Those fifteen hours were governed by the supreme logic of triage, where the focus was singular: Get this baby out of me, safely.

To that end, the two doctors took turns reaching deep into my uterus, grabbing onto my child's tiny shoulders, and attempting to pull her out of an opening in my flesh only centimeters wide. Each time it felt like their arms were ripping me apart from within. They told me to push. I pushed. It didn't feel like anything was moving. "I thought for sure you were going to need a C-section," Mom told me later, when it was all over. "Their arms were inside you up to their elbows. I watched the whole thing. It was the scariest moment of my life."

When people tell you that you don't feel childbirth with an epidural, are they intentionally lying? Or are they referring only to the contractions? I agree that I did not feel any of those after I got the anesthesia. Or is a normal, healthy birth, in which a baby is ready and willing to come out, in which a baby is seven pounds instead of one, in which a baby is alive, actually less physically painful than what I experienced?

Because the pain I felt was violent and excruciating. The two doctors would force their hands deeper into me and my body would instinctively retreat, my legs instinctively pushing them out, these benevolent intruders, these vicious saviors. Gabe would remind me, gently, not to pull away, and I would muster the courage to let them in. At some point it became too painful. They stopped, asked W to order a dose of intravenous morphine. They fed it through my veins and immediately asked if I felt anything. I said I didn't. A few seconds later, I felt a warmth spread outward from my center. I smiled (goofily, Gabe said) and told them never mind, I felt it.

It still hurt, but I guess less? I let them push further, and then I felt again that I needed to use the bathroom. I told the doctors this. They said it was okay if I did, just focus on pushing. I focused on pushing. Maybe a minute later, I felt something. I would have bet a hundred dollars that I'd pooped.

I said, "What was that?"

Doctor R said, "That was your daughter."

The relief felt like another dose of painkillers coursing through me, turning off every muscle I hadn't known I was clenching, hard. I asked if she was okay, which now makes me want to cry. The nurses were going to clean her up, Doctor R said. They would bring her back to me in a minute.

Until then, the work wasn't done. There was still the placenta, which is supposed to detach on its own, but this is less likely at twenty-two weeks than it is at forty. Doctor R instructed the male doctor to go in and get it. This didn't feel so much painful as absolutely insane, wild and disgusting, like a foreign body was being exorcized from my gut, causing a rippling shudder through my abdomen. It was over within seconds, and the doctor reported that he'd gotten everything. It was a few minutes after six a.m. on February 1, 2023, and I was empty.

Anumber of times throughout that final week in January, the option had been presented to Gabe and me to take a photo with Simone. There were professional services with names like Now I Lay Me Down to Sleep that would memorialize child loss in a high-quality portrait. With all respect to parents who choose to go this route, it felt wrong for us. A posed photo would be too macabre, an iPhone photo too trivial. We'd never forget what she looked like, we said.

I don't regret this decision. I wouldn't want to have an image right now to look at, a visual crutch that could only ever have been an approximation of all that she was, might have been. What I do regret is that in the few minutes I had to hold my daughter in my arms, I obeyed the doctors who told me not to unwrap her from the blanket they'd hidden her in, that I allowed myself to be dissuaded from seeing all of her, from touching her hands, from kissing her toes, from feeling the strong little body that I felt so powerfully, undeniably, was a part of mine.

That when the nurse told me it was time, I listened. That I gave my child to her, this trustworthy professional, to usher her into the realm of the dead.

That from that moment until Gabe handed me the white porcelain urn that held her remains a week later, I did not know where my daughter was.

That I failed in my solemn duty as a parent to take care of her. As in life, so in death.

That I did not cremate her with my own two hands.

Of course I know that regrets are useless, and delusional. Nothing I'd done in those first days of February, no amount of time I'd had with Simone's lifeless form, would have felt like enough. But that doesn't mean it's not deeply unnatural, this way we have of mediating our contact with the dead. Of dealing with mortality by not dealing with it at all.

A month and a half later, on a visit to North Carolina in late March, my mother and I were driving to a deli to pick up sandwiches. I can't remember the exact context of the conversation, but we were remembering the day of Simone's birth, and she told me in the car that before they brought Simone to me, a nurse had warned her how difficult it might be to take her back from my arms. "If it becomes a problem," the nurse had said, "we'll just say that we have to take the baby back to clean her. That can make the separation easier."

But I hadn't made it a problem. I had handed over my child with my usual deference to authority, not questioning whether there were, or should be, another way. To tell you the truth, though I can't forget what it felt like to hold her, somehow I don't remember the exact moment she left my arms. I don't re-member acknowledging in my mind that it would be the last time I ever touched her.

What I do remember is that a little while later, maybe min-utes, maybe hours, when I was still in the hospital bed, I asked to hold her again. In that car ride with my mother in March, she told me it still made her cry to think about.

"You weren't angry," she remembered. "You were beseeching the nurse just to bring her back to you for one more minute. You said, 'I only want to hold her one more time. I promise I'll give her back to you.' It broke my heart."

We were both crying by the time I pulled into the deli's gravel parking lot. Who gave the poor nurse the orders to tell me no?

The rest of Simone's "birthday," a cold and sunny Wednesday, is hazy to me now.

W came in to say her shift was ending, she would be going home. She said she hoped to see me again, back on this floor, under better circumstances, sometime in the future. A new nurse came in, M, and she was peppy and talked a lot.

Mom and Tom walked up the street to Lexington Candy Shop for breakfast, and brought food back for Gabe and me. I think Gabe got an egg sandwich. I had a Greek omelet with rye toast, and ate it greedily.

One by one, over the next couple hours, the tethers I had to that hospital room came off: the IV, the catheter, the epidural needle, the heart rate monitor.

Doctor B came by to visit, and to check how I was doing. He told me he would let me know the results of the biopsy within a couple of weeks. I cried as I thanked him for everything.

I texted the group chat that she'd been born. Simone Liu Bump, one pound two ounces, thirty centimeters long. "She had no heartbeat," I wrote, "but the biggest fiercest heart I've ever felt. I love you all so much." In the coming days I would use these exact words over and over in texts and emails to everyone I knew, feeling the need to make sure the world knew she existed.

From the hospital bed, I also texted my father, who'd called to see how I was doing a few days earlier, not yet knowing about Simone's condition. "I'm in the hospital," I wrote, "the baby didn't make it." The distance this oversimplification put between us hurt me, but the only people I needed in that moment were my mother and my husband. I was also unsure of how my dad—who'd been raised Mormon, left the church in his twenties, and since had a relationship with the church I couldn't quite track—might judge my "choice" to terminate, which I'd have done anything not to choose. I know now that I was projecting my own guilt onto him, and onto anyone whom I suspected might possibly confirm it. (Weeks later he would tell me that, as a pure conservative, he detested government interference, including in healthcare.)

The nurse navigator had been in and out of the room so many times throughout the previous afternoon and night and morning, checking on me, checking on my family, sitting on my bed and talking. This morning she came in with a bag from Target from which she pulled out two sports bras, one gray and one black, in a size extra-small, which was not my size. "They're supposed to be tight," she said. "Put one on and do not take it off, ever, not when you sleep, not when you shower. When the placenta detaches, your hormones send a signal to your breasts to start producing milk. You can prevent that by constricting the glands and avoiding any contact with them whatsoever."

At some point I said I had to pee, and started to get up, and at least two people rushed to my side to stop me. "Easy, easy," the nurse navigator said. "You trying to run a marathon? You haven't stood up in twenty-four hours. I'll help you."

She walked me into the bathroom and stood outside. She asked if I was okay. I said I was, but that there was a lot of blood, and because the epidural was starting to wear off, I now felt very tender and sore. "Can I come in?" she asked gently. She brought me a clear squeeze bottle that looked like it was for condiments at a diner, except it was filled with warm water. She used it to soothe wounds I didn't know I had, and then helped me into an adult diaper with a little purple bow on the front that I actually thought looked kind of cute, like boy shorts. I hugged her goodbye.

I went home. I wanted to walk, it was nice out and my mom lived only eight blocks from the hospital, but everyone looked at me like I was insane. "Give it a couple of days before you start walking around," M said. "And no strenuous exercise or sex for six weeks. The bleeding should not last that long, and it should gradually get lighter and lighter," she continued. "If it gets worse or you feel severe cramping, call Doctor R." I asked how bad "severe" was. She said, "You'll know."

I changed into the too-tight sports bra and pulled leggings on over my diaper, feeling self-conscious that you could see its bulk if you looked carefully enough at my butt. I packed the Carmexes I hadn't lost in my backpack with the thick book I had been kidding myself to think I'd be able to read during my stay, and all the pads and ointments and prescription slips for grief counseling they were discharging me with. D came to check on me one last time, and to say goodbye. She gave me her phone number, and I texted her so she had mine. We haven't sent each other a single message since, but it still comforts me to have her name in my phone.

We got home and I took a frustrating shower—sports bra on, trying to clean myself without getting the front of me wet. When I got out I stared at my body in the mirror of my childhood bathroom. It looked the same as it had before I was pregnant, which was depressing. I'd never gotten big enough for stretch marks or loose skin. It would have made more sense to be left with a scar, a visual indicator of how different I was now.

I came downstairs in a fresh diaper underneath my maternity sweatpants and the DAP sweatshirt I'd worn so often in those days, feeling hidden, cocooned in its giant fabric, that it had become mine before Gabe even got to try it on.

I sat with Tom in my mom's dining room and we started an incredibly hard puzzle that was a poster for the Grand Canyon and had broad swaths of different shades of purple and orange and brown. As the epidural continued to wear off I started to feel soreness and pain when I sat down, so I borrowed the donut cushion my grandmother used for her chronic hip pain. It helped, and I carried it around with me, from the puzzle table to the kitchen table to the couch, for days.

Natalie came over again, this time with a box of four giant, scone-sized cookies. We ordered takeout and after dinner we all broke off small pieces of the different cookie flavors: chocolate chip, chocolate chip walnut, chocolate peanut butter, and oatmeal raisin. Eventually crumbs from all four gathered at the bottom of the box and I mixed them into new, smaller cookies between my fingers and ate those. I asked her what she would tell Baldwin; how do you explain such a death to a child, one that happened before birth? He'd known Simone was inside me; how would he understand why she wasn't anymore?

She told me not to worry about Baldwin, that she'd been around his age when her own mother miscarried, and the thing she remembered most was her mother's sadness, rather than the details of what caused it. Baldwin was "much more oriented toward you," she said; for a four-year-old the idea of pregnancy was abstract enough that he would only process my emotions around it.

Still, I thought of what he'd lost too. He has cousins on his dad's side, cousins he sees often and plays with and loves. But he was going to teach Simone, this baby cousin, how to take a bath. How to be a child, and then, eventually, an adult. He had the most life to live without her, and I grieved for him too, however he was able to process the loss.

The days passed, and the only diapers I changed were mine. Liz flew in from San Francisco and she and Tom would go out in the mornings to get fresh bagels for all of us, with small tubs of plain and jalapeño cream cheese. We labored over the Grand Canyon puzzle, Mom and Tom and Liz and I switching seats every so often to work on a different section, me shifting the donut pillow from chair to chair, unable to sit comfortably without it. Liz and Tom organized all the pieces by color and then by shape. They kept referring to one particular shape that looked like it had a little head and long, thin wings as "the Batman one."

At some point that week, Mom came in and told me I needed to pick an urn. She'd been handling all the paperwork for the cremation and funereal services, things I knew would never get done if I didn't have her. I also knew, from when Gong Gong died, and from when her best friend, my godmother, died of cancer a few years before that, that Mom grieves through the completion of small but necessary tasks. She plans memorials, she makes guest lists, she puts decades worth of financial documents in order, she gathers photo montages and sets them to Elton John, she executes wills.

She does these things because she is generous, but also because they calm her. She does them so nobody else has to.

As if I were doing my mother a favor, I grudgingly scrolled through the pdf of the funeral home's catalog of options: wooden boxes in the shape of a cross, decorative hearts in pink and cerulean and red, stone sculptures, even necklaces and clocks. There was a section of smaller vessels specifically designed to hold a baby or child; these were shaped like baby animals or angels, and some had words on them that said something about beautiful lives cut too short.

We were not going to choose any of those. Many of the adult-sized urns also came in smaller versions, and Mom said these were for when the remains of a parent, for example, needed to be divided into smaller portions for multiple siblings. The chamber size of each was listed in cubic inches. I wasn't sure how much volume my dead daughter would take up in ash form.

I told Mom I didn't like any of them. I didn't want to pick one. She did not tell me the truth, that I was acting like a child.

This talk of her physical remains made me realize then that I had no idea where my daughter was now. I had no idea if she'd already been cremated or if her body was still intact, lying in a freezer, one of so many bodies, cold and alone.

"I need to go to the hospital, I need to find her," I said, tears suddenly streaming down my face.

"You can't, sweetie," Mom said, her voice catching.

She was my child, I howled. Her body was my body. How could I have just left it for a stranger to dispose of?

I got up, and then Mom got up, and then Mom held me. Liz and Tom stopped doing the puzzle and just sat there quietly, looking down.

This wasn't my first or last break, but it may have been my worst. For weeks after she was born, I felt intermittent flashes of panic, like I'd forgotten a limb somewhere, left part of me out in the wild, vulnerable and adrift. Maybe the detachment of the placenta from my uterus had also stimulated some animal instinct to protect. Maybe my body still thought there was someone who physically needed me to survive, and it kept reminding me, viscerally and urgently, that I wasn't doing my job.

Right then, I was furious. At myself for having allowed that small body to be somebody else's responsibility besides mine. This had not been my choice to make, but why not? By what authority? Would it have been illegal not to hand her back to the nurse, to refuse to leave her side? Whose law would I have been breaking if I'd unwrapped my daughter from the soft white blanket, kissed every inch of her, of my miracle? If I'd insisted on carrying her to the crematorium myself, to insist to that faceless facility, designed to remain so to the innocent living, that I be the one to transmute her flesh into the ash at my bedside?

Instead, I'd have to pick a painted urn from a pleasant catalog, and try to form some approximate emotional connection to that.

Gabe spent a lot of time in bed those first few days, or in the small gym in the basement of my mom's apartment building, which hardly anybody ever used. When I was in bed with him, we worried over returning to North Carolina, when and how, worried over Hopscotch's neutering appointment, which we'd had to push back because of all this. A lot of the time I would be downstairs with Natalie or Tom or Liz or whoever else had come to see us, and he would be upstairs with my bedroom door closed, sleeping or reading or watching soccer, exhausted and preferring to be alone.

When the situation had still been medical, in Simone's final days, it made sense that the attention was disproportionately on me: my blood pressure, my uterus, my life. But once I was physically safe, we were experiencing the same thing, Gabe and I, the loss of the most important person who'd ever entered either of our lives. It has always been my nature to force other people to know how I feel, to ask for help when I need it and sometimes even when I don't, even if that need can't be met, at least you'll know about it. Though I'd known Gabe was not that way, this period brought that difference into new light.

The general dynamic between us has always been that I panic about something, tell him about it, and he assures me everything is okay. This routine of ours is so natural, so airtight, that when he vomited on the side of the road last summer after drinking an unpasteurized green juice on the way from Healdsburg to San Francisco, I felt not just worried for him, but utterly disoriented to be the one who was okay. I'd leaned so heavily on this unfair ideal of him as healthy and stable that this glimpse of his vulnerability upended my own sense of safety. Vomiting was the worst thing I could imagine, and it was happening to someone I loved; I could bring him Gatorade and one of my trusty Zofrans, but I couldn't make his pain go away. Fortunately, by the next morning he was back to full health and ordered a beef burrito for lunch as if nothing had ever happened. I, on the other hand, can recite every minute of that day as if it were still happening.

All to say, the dynamic had already been established even before pregnancy gave us an excuse to codify it into policy: I was the weak and ailing one, he was the strong and capable one who could take care of us both and then some. Without Simone, I'm not sure I would have been forced to examine this pressure I'd put on him to always be okay. To see that I took up so much of the air in the room with my feelings, my needs, that I might not be leaving enough room for his.

But just seeing a problem doesn't fix it, and in those first days without Simone I struggled to figure out what Gabe needed, besides what I gleaned from his behavior to be peace and quiet. I knew having so many people around could be overwhelming to him sometimes, but I didn't know if that included me too. When I asked him what he needed, I still felt that habitual protector in his voice, like he didn't want to burden me with the answer.

We were an imperfect support system for each other in those

days, weeks, months. One day I'd break down and another day he would, each in our own ways that looked pretty different from each other's, and we just prayed those weren't the same day, the same hour. Someone had to hold it together. It was usually him.

On Friday, two days after Simone was born and three days after she died, the temperature in New York dropped, and Mom, Tom, Liz, Gabe, Natalie, and I went to the Met. I was able to walk by then, but as we turned the corner from a side street onto Fifth Avenue, powerful and freezing-cold winds knocked our hair and hats in odd directions, whipped us mercilessly across the face.

We were there to see *Hear Me Now*, an exhibition of pottery mostly made by the enslaved South Carolina artist David Drake, who was also a poet. Giant clay vessels molded in various shades of glossy brown were housed in glass cases, their white pedestals displaying typed transcriptions of the verses Drake etched into them, working clandestinely and quickly before someone caught him, before his wet scroll dried. His literacy was, of course, a secret, punishable by death.

On one vessel, he'd written:

> *A very Large Jar which has 4 handles =*
> *pack it full of fresh meats—then light candles—*
> *L. m . April 12 . 1858 / Dave*

On another:

> *I wonder where is all my relation*
> *Friendship to all—and every nation*
> *Lm Aug 16 1857 Dave*

I imagined Simone's remains resting forever in an urn like these, her tiny volume leaving ample room in its cavernous interior, room for her to laugh and run, room for her voice to echo against the clay walls, Dave's material, his desperate melody, making it so that wherever I was, I would hear her call.

The exhibition also displayed ceramics by the contemporary artist Simone Leigh. Natalie came over to me and apologized; she hadn't known this show would include her work, and she worried about me seeing this name out in the world. I couldn't imagine being upset by this, and I told her that. I would always be thinking about Simone whether I heard her name or not, and anyway I liked imagining my daughter growing up and moving the world the way Leigh does.

We went to the gift shop and Tom bought me a puzzle, and then we went home and picked an urn from the pdf, a small, white porcelain one with a bird on it.

A couple days later—on the day a 7.8 magnitude earthquake

struck Turkey and Syria and killed tens of thousands of people—for the second time in a month, Gabe and Mom went together to the same funeral home to retrieve the urn that carried Simone's remains. They didn't say, but I assume they had no trouble carrying this one.

On the morning of Saturday, February 11, I was alone in the Boston Common, walking. Gabe had driven us up the previous afternoon, while Jamie drove Mom, Poh Poh, and Liz in a separate car. Uncle Mark had booked us all rooms at the Marriott Copley Place, a towering corporate building where there happened to be a high school Model UN conference that same weekend. Teenagers trolled the multiple lobbies and elevator banks with their Starbucks and their starched suits; at night they ran screaming through the halls, drunk and in trouble, interrupting our sleep, and our grief, with their laughter. Chaperones looked depleted, disgusted. To cover their own asses, they taped the kids' doors from the outside after curfew.

It was around nine a.m. and Gabe had fallen back asleep after waking up too early, as he often does when he's anxious. I changed into a fresh diaper and sweatpants and directed myself to a nearby café. I ordered a latte and a dish that involved an egg and mushrooms and potatoes, and found a seat at a marble counter. I put on my headphones and googled "memoir about child loss."

A lot of titles came up. Some of them were billed as self-help, written, I supposed, exactly for people like me, to make us feel like someone had answers. I am sure these books are helpful. I did not click on them.

Instead I downloaded an audiobook called *An Exact Replica of a Figment of My Imagination*, written and read by the writer Elizabeth McCracken, whom I knew as an author of fiction. I had not heard of this memoir. The cover showed a bright aquamarine wall with a faint rainbow of light refracted into a corner. It made me think of the slivers of light I saw in the mornings or afternoons, coming in through openings in our windows or the trees, projecting a contained bit of glitter on a wall of our home, how I associated those apparitions with my bright Simone.

I started listening to this audiobook as my eggs came. They were runny, though I'd asked for them fully cooked. This used to scare me, the prospect of salmonella, even long before I was pregnant. The potatoes and mushrooms were in some kind of thick, creamy broth that was rich and suddenly nauseating to me. But nothing mattered now, and I ate it all.

"A child dies in this book: a baby," McCracken spoke into my ear as I sat at the marble countertop watching an employee prepare steamed milk for someone's cappuccino. "You don't have to tell me how sad that is."

I finished my food and walked toward the park, still listening. McCracken had met the writer Edward Carey in her late thirties, and become pregnant. For some reason they were living in the French countryside, and they were ecstatic. The baby was a boy, and they referred to him throughout the pregnancy as Pudding.

I reached the edge of the Common and turned left, circling the perimeter clockwise. The night before, Gabe and Jamie and I had done a similar walk in the other direction, Jamie guiding us through the city where he'd graduated from college two years earlier, the two of them now and again drifting ahead of me, their long legs carrying them quicker than I could manage. I'd hang back and listen to the muffle of their voices, wishing they'd wait up, wishing I could tell them how much I loved them, how badly I needed their radiant, unapologetic health, their stupid jokes.

In late April 2006, McCracken found out that Pudding had no heartbeat. She gave birth to him without her husband in the room; she wanted it this way. She held her dead baby in her arms, and then he was displaced by the *"certificat d'enfant sans vie*, certificate of the birth of a child without life—birth certificate, death certificate, whatever you want to call it."

As I walked along the street where Jamie had pointed out to us the bar from *Cheers*, where we'd Zillow-ed gigantic brick town houses lit warmly from the inside, I looked to my right, into the park, and saw a pond with some geese around it. I walked through the gates and along a path until I got to a bench at the edge of the water. It was freezing, but I remembered the summer day, it must have been thirty years before, when my grandfather had taken me on a boat ride on this same pond, where the boat had had a large swan statue on the back of it, and I'd thrown a massive, depraved tantrum. The way my grandmother told the story, Gong Gong was struck dumb by my shrieking and flailing, unsure what to say or do, so he said and did nothing.

What I think now is that he didn't find it that alarming at all, a child fussing, and that he forgave me, his Guai Guai, and he knew my pain would pass.

These boats were a tourist attraction; there had been many other people on the boat. I didn't find them there now, it made sense they wouldn't run in February. I took a picture of the pond and sent it to my mom and grandmother. "I can picture Simone having a tantrum on a swan boat with Gong Gong now ♥."

I kept walking, I kept listening. "The baby was dead, but he still had to be born," McCracken said, like she was dragging my own heart out into the cold winter air, asking me to look at it.

"I don't want those footprints framed on the wall, but I don't want to hide them beneath the false bottom of a trunk. I don't want to wear my heart on my sleeve or put it away in cold storage. I don't want to fetishize, I don't want to repress, I want his death to be what it is: a fact."

I thought of Simone's footprints, not an inch long, on the small white card inside the small white envelope a nurse had handed to us to hold in place of our daughter, an envelope that also contained a card with their condolences, and the small white hat Simone had worn. "The ink pad we had was dry," the doctor had explained, "so we had to run around finding a new one." I thanked her and wondered how infrequently they made cards like this. The prints were asymmetrical, and the ink didn't seem to have made it onto all her toes. Everything else I saw of her was Gabe, but her feet, narrow and long, were mine.

On the other side of the card there was a leaf, along with the following chart, filled out by hand:

> Baby's Name: *Simone Liu Bump*
> Birth Date: *February 1st 2023 @ 6:10am*
> Baby's Birth Weight: *1* lbs. *2* oz.
> Baby's Length: *30 cm*

McCracken also said, "No more talk of angels."

I let myself back into our hotel room to find Gabe showered and dressed in a black jacket and pants. I told him I'd found another person who understood. Elizabeth McCracken, had he read her work? He had, only her stories. I told him she'd spoken from within me. I took a shower and put on a black turtleneck sweater dress and black tights. You couldn't really tell that it was a maternity dress, but it hid me capably.

Because of a logistical family-group-chat snafu, we had to pile seven of us into Gabe's car, my brother and cousins and our partners, for the twenty-minute drive to Bernard's. When we arrived at the restaurant these same six people circled me in the bar area, protecting me from having to speak to anyone. I said muffled hellos to my grandparents' friends and former colleagues, relics of their younger life, mostly older Chinese people whom I felt reasonably certain had no idea what had happened to me, and some younger family and friends who definitely did. Everybody I talked to said they were sorry for my loss, and I couldn't always be sure which one they meant.

I sat at the kids' table, which happened to be the exact table where I'd sat at Gong Gong's ninetieth, less than four years and yet a literal lifetime ago. Waiters brought dish after dish, Peking duck with scallions and smoked chicken and noodles and gai lan with plump shiitake mushrooms. When I declined a serving of the shrimp in a thick white sauce, Jamie said loudly, "What's wrong, Lauren, you don't want to try the creamy seafood?"

Throughout the meal people went up to a microphone to give speeches according to a program carefully designed in the previous weeks by my family, in a series of heated emails I only foggily comprehended. Liz and Caroline got up to speak on behalf of the grandchildren, then two different Bobs, a woman who'd worked for the commercial architecture firm my grandfather cofounded who said he'd supported her when she fought for the company to introduce paid maternity leave in the '80s.

One man I'd never met before got up and introduced himself as one of the guys Gong Gong used to play tennis with every week. With impressive dramatic effect, he related a story my grandmother had told many times, of when Gong Gong was a teenager in Hong Kong under Japanese occupation, conning a Japanese telephone company into believing he was old enough to employ so he could support himself and his grandmother with sacks of rice they could then barter for more substantial food. One day, on his way home from work, he found a baby on the street.

He looked around for this child's parents for hours, thinking they might soon come back from wherever they'd had to go without him. No one came, and the curfew was approaching, he had to get home to his grandmother. He was barely a teenager, barely able to feed himself and his grandmother, let alone a stranger's baby.

"What would you do?" this tennis friend posed to the audience, silent except for chopsticks clinking on plates.

My grandfather took this boy in, named himself responsible for another person's life, and figured out how to keep him alive for days or weeks as he posted signs all over his route to work in case the child's parents were alive and looking for him.

They were, and they found Gong Gong, and Gong Gong said goodbye to the child. I imagined the moment when my grandfather, a child himself, had to hand over this baby he hadn't had for very long. This baby he'd nurtured, shared a shelter and probably a bed with, for as long as time would let them have together. It turned out that the boy belonged to a family of successful sea merchants. Gong Gong handed them back their child, and asked for nothing in return.

I cried several times throughout this lunch, for my grandfather who was known to so many, his boyish smile projected onto a large screen, at five and thirty-one and ninety-three; for Simone, who never got to smile at all. My grandmother had been surprised that I felt up to going to this event, had told me several times that she would understand if I wasn't well enough, I needed to rest. But I said it wasn't like this was a wedding. I didn't have to dance, or have fun, or even really talk. It was a sad occasion, and sad was the one thing I felt I could do.

At the end of the meal, as waiters served heaping platters of cut fruit—my grandfather's nightly favorite, chocolate ice cream, had been vetoed by my grandmother, who was always monitoring Gong Gong's diet, even in death—my mom stood up to

close out the event. She called him "beatific," optimistic, steady.
She spoke to his patience and attention to detail, his gratitude for
every single day he lived, from his war-stricken childhood to his
adulthood designing giant glass towers that still dot the Boston
skyline. She talked about her own gratitude for the years she got
to live with him at the end of his life, got to prepare two scoops
of Ben & Jerry's Chocolate Fudge Brownie ice cream in a stale
supermarket wafer cone for him every single night, to which he
always, always responded with a child's unjaded glee: "Oh!
Thank you!" She spoke about the time Park Avenue was shut
down to traffic, and so they got to do their daily walk around
the block in the middle of the street. "He kept saying, 'I can't
believe it,'" she remembered. "Every day was the most exciting
day of his life."

She closed with something about how my grandfather's name
meant "bright star," and how he was hers. She was in tears, and
so was most of the room. The run of show had been carefully
planned on one heated email chain: Who would be asked to
speak, in what order, for how long. Who went by Bob, and who
went by Robert. According to this plan, Mom was supposed to
go last, thank everyone for coming.

But this wasn't the end. As if she had only half-heard her
daughter's poignant tribute, Poh Poh jolted up, all ninety pounds
of her, small and birdlike and more adorable than I remembered
ever finding her before. She pounded over to the microphone so
quickly she'd forgotten about her walker.

"Just a minute," she said, exasperated. "I forgot about Yu Sing's
Chinatown colleagues." Before cofounding Jung | Brannen, he'd
worked with a team of pro bono architects to build a commun-

ity center for the elderly in Chinatown. "Paul, are you here? Could you speak?"

Poor Paul, unprepared for this address, took it like a champ. From the table next to mine, a small man stood up with his iPhone dangling from a string around his neck and spoke from the heart about this community center.

His address became the day's new ending, unplanned and awkward.

Gabe, Jamie, Liz, Caroline, Sebastian, Sam, and I all went around the corner for ice cream. We were extremely full, but our excuse was that it was "for Gong Gong." The cold morning had given in to a bright and sunny afternoon, and the air felt refreshing after being crammed in the restaurant.

Even fuller, we drove back to the hotel and Gabe and I fell asleep for a couple of hours.

That night, Jamie made a reservation for the whole family at a barbecue restaurant downtown. He said it was near the federal courthouse Gong Gong and his firm had designed right on the harbor, completed in 1999. My brother had studied architecture at BU, and he'd written a paper on this building senior year. On the walk over, Mom overheard him telling Sebastian that he'd gone back to read his paper that afternoon, to refresh his memory before giving us this "tour."

Dinner was at a long table in the middle of a busy dining room, loud and chill, and afterward we walked in groups of two or three through the cold harbor air, Jamie leading us past several blocks and a park chained up at night. Everyone was freezing by the time we rounded a corner and saw it, the majestic, curved façade of glass windows, its arc geometrically smooth, spooned by a more traditional-looking brick structure with horizontal granite trim and grand archways carved out over a walkway on street level.

I don't know what I'd expected, maybe a regular building. I didn't expect to see my grandfather written into space: placid, imperturbable, infinitely stable, supportive in a way that begged no thanks. Elegant and dignified, not a hair out of place.

In this building, reflecting lights from the moon and the skyline onto us and the water behind; in the faces of my brother and my mother beholding it, the faces of my husband and my cousins and my uncle and all their spouses, I saw everyone who was still here, and those who weren't. I saw the lives I could still feel in my hand and knew that we were not everything, but we were enough.

Outside the door of my hospital room at Lenox Hill, someone had hung a plaque, a small tile, painted with an orchid and raindrops. My mother told me this months later, at her kitchen table. She'd seen it as she and Tom and Gabe stood outside my closed door, listening to my wails as the epidural needle threaded through a nerve in my spine. She thought they'd hung it so nobody in the hospital, rushing through whatever rounds they had to do, accidentally walked into my room without knowing the baby being delivered in there was already dead.

As with the blue-trimmed tiles in the first home she brought me to, I never saw this tile either, this functioning symbol of my sorrow, this warning to all who might be expecting happiness not to seek that in here, not now.

I know there will be happiness again, in whatever form it happens to take. In the beginning of my life without Simone, when I stopped bleeding, when all that was physically left of my pregnancy was a vicious pain in my lower back that signaled the lingering obliteration of my abdominal wall, I felt something like survivor's guilt. How had I managed to survive intact when this body who had been not just a part of me, but all of me, my whole future, was in ashes?

"Lighter things will happen to you," a stranger tells Mc-Cracken early in the book, "and your child will still be dead, and you will spend your life trying to resolve this."

I will spend my life comparing every minute to the corresponding one in the parallel universe where Simone got to live: Now I would be twenty-two weeks pregnant; everyone at the memorial service would notice my belly and politely congratulate me, taking note of the solemn march of time: a ninety-four-year-old man leaving this earth, his great-granddaughter taking her place in it.

Now I would be forty weeks, experiencing labor for the first time, gratefully blind to the truth that such grueling effort could have any other outcome than joy.

Now she would be a month old, my mother coming to live with us for weeks, maybe my brother too would come visit, and Natalie, Tom and Debbie, Mike, Liz, Caroline. I would be exhausted, I would be frustrated, maybe even depressed. No matter what I felt, though, she would reach for me every day, helpless and hungry.

Now she'd be four, trying on sneakers at Fleet Feet on Franklin, Gabe tying them up for her and pressing his thumb to her toes that look so much like mine, asking her where they begin, if this pair is too big, or too small.

Now she'd be eleven or thirteen or twenty, telling me all the ways in which I am lame, in which I've hurt her. All the times I have not shown up for her as she needed me to.

These moments all belong to what a new, very pregnant friend recently termed my "ghost life." It's not that it never got to happen, or that I'd imagined it in my head. It was realer than anything I've ever experienced, and then it died.

A lot of things happen to the living, and this is just one of them. Nothing good came out of it, and it didn't happen for any reason. The world does not care what we think about it. By the luck of the draw, I get to keep living, and I know better than to say that's not a miracle. More things will happen to me before I die, and some of them will even be good. None of them will be her.

I'm not sure if Simone can hear me, where she is right now, where Gong Gong is, where I will go when I die, if all of these are somehow the same place, together. But still, when I see the little sliver of light on my bedroom wall, I feel her there, her little hand, fingers clenching and extending, her fierce grip telling me, It's okay. I'm okay.

acknowledgments

Thank you to Bill Clegg, Scott Moyers, Helen Rouner, Yuki Hirose, Allison King, Juliana Kiyan, Jessie Stratton, and the whole team at Penguin Press for making this book possible, and for your great care in the process. Thank you to my *Book Review* family for the support I needed and then some. Thank you to Gabe, my first and most important reader. Thank you to Mom for more things than I can name. Simone and Noah, it is all for you.